PACIFY ME

PACIFY ME

A Handbook for the Freaked-Out New Dad

CHRIS MANCINI

SIMON SPOTLIGHT ENTERTAINMENT

New York   London   Toronto   Sydney

S|S|E

SIMON SPOTLIGHT ENTERTAINMENT
A Division of Simon & Schuster, Inc.
1230 Avenue of the Americas
New York, NY 10020

First Simon Spotlight Entertainment trade paperback edition June 2009

SIMON SPOTLIGHT ENTERTAINMENT and colophon are trademarks
of Simon & Schuster, Inc.

For information about special discounts for bulk purchases, please contact
Simon & Schuster Special Sales at 1-866-506-1949 or
business@simonandschuster.com.

The Simon & Schuster Speakers Bureau can bring authors to your live event. For
more information or to book an event, contact the Simon & Schuster Speakers
Bureau at 1-866-248-3049 or visit our website at www.simonspeakers.com.

Designed by Dana Sloan

Manufactured in the United States of America

3   5   7   9   10   8   6   4   2

Library of Congress Cataloging-in-Publication Data
Mancini, Chris.
Pacify me : a handbook for the freaked-out new dad / by Chris Mancini.
p. cm.
1. Fatherhood—United States—Humor. 2. Fathers—United
States—Humor. 3. Father and infant. I. Title.
HQ756.M33 2009
649'.10851—dc22
                                      2009004761

ISBN 978-1-4391-2887-9
ISBN 978-1-4391-3735-2 (ebook)

To Audrey and Isabella,
who showed me what I was missing

Contents

CONTENTS

Foreword

by Stefanie Wilder-Taylor

When my friend Chris told me he was writing a book for expectant fathers on how they really feel about becoming a dad, I was like, "Whaaa?" and then I think I said something along the lines of "But guys don't even read any of those new mom books." To which he replied something like "That's because they're all directed at women. They don't appeal to men. It's not like we guys don't have anxieties and worries about impending fatherhood. Our fears are just different. And we're easily bored. I've yet to see a book truly address a guy's point of view with any sort of humor." Okay, it's possible that I added a lot more details to this conversation, but he did say he was writing a book for dads and that there aren't any good ones out there—*that* much I'm sure about. And he had a point. We women collect the new mommy tomes by the tens of thousands. The very second we find out we're knocked up, we're logging onto BabyCenter to find out what's happening with our embryo every second of every day. We wait impatiently for our weekly update from the website alerting us that our previously lentil bean–size baby-to-be has finally moved on to chickpea status. While we wait, we're raiding book stores by day and perusing Amazon using the key word "pregnancy" by night.

True story: Not too long ago, my sister-in-law who was trying to get pregnant asked if she could borrow my copy of *What to Expect When You're Expecting*. I said, "Geez, you're not even pregnant! Slow down. This is the part where you're still having sex. Hopefully you don't need a book for that (although there are some good ones out there)." She wanted to know what to expect while she was planning on at some point expecting. Women are crazy. But you didn't need me to tell you that.

If you're reading this book, you're well aware of it—especially because if you're reading this book, your wife or girlfriend is probably pregnant—which everyone knows (except, of course, the pregnant woman) has a tendency to make women insane, frustrating, easily irritated, hot messes with bad skin. But please don't tell her I said that. For your own safety.

The point of the matter is that women want to be experts on what is happening to their body and what is going to happen to their life once they have this baby. We hope to have gleaned enough information to truly have a leg up on the whole experience before it happens, and although we wish that our partner would be as fascinated by every kick, skin splotch, food craving, nursery knickknack, and childproofing seminar as we are, we're usually disappointed.

Close to my due date in my first pregnancy, my husband and I were on our way to a restaurant for what we figured to be one of our last outings as a twosome. While my husband drove, I tried to get him to listen to a passage in one of my numerous pregnancy reference books from a chapter called something like "For the Husband." I figured, since it was aimed directly at him, he might feel more included in the whole "reading everything I can get my hands on" process. Not so much.

Looking back, it was written by a woman and fairly patronizing. There was a lot of "your wife will probably be unpredictable," "try buying her flowers to help her feel appreciated," plenty of "you are an important part of the process!" and not one science fiction reference. My husband pretended to listen, while simultaneously passing slow cars on the freeway, fiddling with the car stereo, and digging through the glove compartment for a Replacements CD because he didn't appreciate the John Mayer CD I'd left in the player. It didn't capture his attention in the least and I, in my pregnant, neurotic, fearful haze, thought he just wasn't that interested and didn't care about being prepared nearly as much as I did.

I was half right. He wasn't interested in the book, but he was quite interested in impending fatherhood. Yet his worries and expectations were not the same as mine and giving him a lone chapter in a woman's book wasn't going to cut it for him.

Men and women experience pregnancy and parenthood differently—starting with the fact that men can drink during and take antidepressants those first endless nine months—but I'm not bitter. It turns out that men worry a whole lot about how much their life is going to change, about how much their *partner* is going to change. Truthfully, I wish my husband had *Pacify Me* before I had our baby, but I also wish *I* had the book before giving birth because I don't think I had any real idea of what he was going through. And at the time the only way to get that information would have been to have a conversation about his feelings. That just seems extreme.

An added benefit of this book, besides showing men that they are not alone with straight lighthearted guy talk and plenty of *Star Wars* references, is that women will love it too. Women love nothing more than to try and figure out what a man is thinking. We can and *have* spent half our young adulthood trying to answer the question "Why hasn't he called?" This book is like a window into a normal man's brain. Does he give a shit about the nursery theme? No. Is he scared you won't want to have sex ever again? Yes. Is he as concerned about finding the best daycare as you are? Actually, hell yes.

Men, you will have fun reading the experience of another guy who is funny, real, entertaining (I've seen him perform in Vegas—trust me, he's hilarious), honest, and thoughtful going through his wife's pregnancy, childbirth, and beyond. But, when you're done, please pass the book on to your partner because she just may love it as much, if not *more*, than you.

So good luck, and may the force be with everyone—or however it goes.

My Life Is Over

That's it. It's done. Finito. Stick a fork in me. Game over, man. The Fat Lady has sung. *My life is over.* It's the first thought that came into my head when I learned I was going to be a father. All of a sudden I knew my life was *never* going to be the same. No more doing what I wanted when I wanted. No more freedom. No more all-night *Halo* playing, no more going out with the guys, and no more eating pancakes whenever I wanted to. My life from that point on would be endless responsibility and child care. Baby food, crying, PTA meetings, and ballet recitals. I didn't *want* to go to the ballet! I hate ballet! Seriously, does anyone *really* like ballet? The flash of life ahead was making me feel light-headed.

I was never against having kids. My wife, Audrey, and I talked about it before we got married. I always wanted them eventually. But suddenly, eventually came. I had just gotten used to being an adult. My wife may debate this, since I said for my birthday I wanted either the new *Resident Evil* game or *Aqua Teen Hunger Force* on DVD, so I suppose it's relative. But now I had to be a father too?! I felt like the clock started ticking and time was running out. It's like I was caught in some kind of pre-parental *Logan's Run*.

So does any of the above sound at all familiar to you? I thought so. Think of it as a knee-jerk reaction to something so huge that your brain can't even fully comprehend it. Don't worry; eventually it will sink in. Usually after the baby is about six months old. Your brain will finally process everything and you'll realize that the scary infant-crying sound *is coming from inside the house*!

So when you crawl out of your full fetal position from under the bed, know and understand that what you're feeling is *perfectly normal*. You're going to feel nervous, anxious, depressed, and uneasy all at once. Like you just ate a chili dog at a Céline Dion concert. Heck, you're going to be feeling so many different things, you may even invent a few new negative emotions of your own. Hyperanxiepression, anyone?

As anxious and nervous as men get when they are about to become fathers, I think I personally raised the bar for pre-baby anxiety. I couldn't eat. I couldn't sleep. I had big whiny fits and eventually I ended up in a psychiatrist's office. Have you noticed that no one ever "goes" to a psychiatrist's office? Everyone just "ends up" there. Like it's a big mystery how it happened. "Huh, how did I get here? And why are there bugs crawling all over me?" Also, a psychiatrist is the one who's a medical doctor. I think if you see the words "Life Coach" on any therapist's wall you should run away, very quickly. I'm pretty sure a life coach is just one step above "Dog Whisperer." Or maybe below.

So after I "ended up" at the psychiatrist's office, I just opened the floodgates. I told him that I didn't want to have a kid, but I *wanted* to want to have a kid. He may have rolled his eyes and checked to see what my co-pay was at that point, but I'm not sure. This whole baby thing was tearing me apart inside. Some mornings it got so bad that I would wake up shaking. "So what should I do, doc? What's wrong with me?" My psychiatrist paused and looked at me patiently. It looked like he was about to lay a secret on me. All right, let's hear it. I was waiting.

Well, he let me in on a secret, all right.

My psychiatrist was kind enough to inform me that these days it's all about mood-elevating drugs and not so much about talking through your problems anymore. So in other words, he was saying that it really didn't matter what either of us said, as long as he had his prescription pad handy. Wow. Does anyone else know about this?

Think about all the wasted years of medical school this knowledge would save! I think that's the subject of another book. Maybe Tom Cruise could write it. Anyway, so my dealer, er, psychiatrist, then listened impatiently to my baby terrification problems and promptly prescribed some Zoloft.

Interestingly, the drugs worked great. I felt better. When you're on antidepressants/anxiety medication, everything's . . . cool. Nothing's too horrible, and nothing's too great. You're Even Steven. Win the lottery? Coool . . . Your car is stolen? Coool . . .

Anyway, the psychiatrist sessions continued, and I got all of my insurance money's worth. We talked about everything from my relationships to my career to my childhood. Sometimes it's easier to talk to a stranger, especially if you know he isn't really listening. Despite his professional opinion, talking about it really did make me feel a little better.

The most ridiculous thing is that it never occurred to me that other fathers-to-be go through and share the same anxieties. In my bubble I thought I was the first man ever to be freaked out about having a child. I don't know why I felt that way, but I did. Maybe it's because we men don't communicate and share feelings with each other the way women do. If we did, well, then we would be women, I suppose. So I'm hoping if I write it down, it will sound less . . . girly. The truth is, *most* guys are terrified of having a child and share the same feelings of nervousness, anxiety, and powerlessness. Even that happy, excited guy handing out cigars is secretly wondering if he'll ever get to go to a restaurant again that doesn't have an arcade attached. If I could give you a hug right now, I would. Seriously, though, ask your friends with kids how they felt beforehand. But make sure you do it in a loud bar over some good manly beers. Domestic!

Look, you *should* be freaked out about having a child. It's huge. I'm not trying to downplay it at all. At this point I'm not even going to tell you to calm down. Go ahead, freak out. Get it all out now. I'm going to repeat this because it's important: *It's perfectly normal to be freaked out about having a child*. After you're done, then calm down. Feel better? No? Don't worry; you will in time.

I'll tell you, I'm more concerned about the guys who *aren't* freaked out about having a child. They're the ones who everyone should be worried about. What's going on in the guy's head who is completely unaffected by impending fatherhood? What's got *him* so preoccupied? That's the same guy who is usually described later on a police report as always being "such a nice, quiet boy."

So here's the deal: This book is all about explaining to you what I went through, what I learned, and why it's not as bad as you think. In other words, I'll be talking you down from the ledge. Because when I was up on that ledge myself, it was a horrible, anxious feeling, but it had a nice view. I'll let you know what I saw.

There were times when I didn't really think I could do it. But I did. And you will too. No matter your starting point, you just may surprise yourself as to how well you'll rise to the occasion. Luke Skywalker started out as a farmer, and look how well he did. Sure, he lost a hand along the way, but there's going to have to be a few small sacrifices.

I'll try to give you an idea of what to expect and how you can avoid a lot of the pitfalls I already fell into for you. I'll be sharing my lessons learned, offer advice, and will give you my opinions and judgments, mainly because I'm very opinionated and judgmental. You'll see.

2

Why Are Men so Freaked Out About Having Children?

D on't get me wrong, some men aren't. They really want to have kids right away and start a family. Most don't. If you are one of the guys who can't wait to have a child, give this book to one of your friends and go to Babies "R" Us right now and fill out your registry.

So why? Why are most of us so afraid and apprehensive about having a child? Other than the obvious reason that it clearly looks like a huge hassle.

I figured it out.

Having a child is the only thing in our entire lives that is *permanent*. Everything else you can get out of: a house, a marriage, a car, a job, etc. We can always sell the house, get a divorce, quit a job, run off and join the circus, etc. Even if we have no intention of leaving, men always like to have an escape plan. No matter how happy we are, there is always that little man in the iron mask in our heads going, "OK, so this is great and all, but when are we getting out of here?" There's nothing we can do about it. This need for a Plan B is genetically programmed into us, like hunting, gathering, and thinking that Michael Bublé is a horrible, talentless hack.

Before I go any further, don't even try to explain this whole escape route thing to your wife. Women *never* understand this. My wife, not following the logic, said, "If you can get out of being married, you can get out of having a child." (Her point was that they are equally important.) No, wrong. You *can* get out of a marriage. You can't get out of having a child. You can only *leave* a child. You've brought this life into this world and you're responsible for it. Everything else was already here when we arrived, including our wives. That's different. We can't be held responsible for anything that came before us.

The other reason men are unnerved about having a child may be generational. Every generation has slightly different priorities and values from the one preceding it. During the '80s and '90s it was mostly about "me." I believe all that crap about listening to our *inner child* may have been taken a little too seriously. We didn't just listen to our inner child, we put him in charge. For better or for worse, we've let that little arrested developmental Napoleon run things. We never got the loose freedom of the '60s and '70s; we just got the consequences. So our way of staying young and free was having a generational Peter Pan complex as seen in every Adam Sandler movie. But we did eventually have to grow up, sort of, but that inner child still defines us. So what happens when that Inner Child has a Child? The obvious: We freak out. I remember a line from BBC's *Coupling* when one of the girls, Susan, got pregnant. She said to the father, "Time's up, Steve. I think it's time for someone else to be the child." Indeed.

Really, there is a bit of a silver lining to this fear-and-anxiety cloud. Contrary to popular opinion, or female opinion, guys deep down really want to do the right thing. We know how permanent having a child is. We recognize the inherent responsibility it brings. And we truly want to make sure we're ready for it. Hell, we have enough trouble with pets and plants.

"Honey? Where's my plant? And where's the cat?"

"Um . . . I'll be right back."

You get the idea. But my wife and I were way beyond cats and ferns at this point. As things continued to ramp up on the baby highway, my anxiety about having a child continued. The Zoloft hadn't really kicked in yet. It needed time to build up in my system, which was kind of scary when I thought about all the *other things* that had probably already built up in my system. Things like caffeine, chocolate-chip cookies, high fructose corn syrup, and a slow, building tolerance for the occasional VH1 reality show. Nothing I'm proud of.

Before the drug worked its magic, my anxiety and depression got worse and I started experiencing some *physical* symptoms, like tightness in my chest. So I went to my real, general practice doctor to see if there was anything wrong with me. Well, that modern medicine could address, anyway. He did lots of tests, took a chest X-ray, and examined me. Then he brought me into his office and gave me the results. Turns out physically I was fine; it was just more stress from having a child on the way. My doctor is a bit of an older guy. That day he looked at me sagely and smiled, like he had seen this scenario many times before. Then he said something really profound to me: "No man wants a child until it's in his arms." I had to think about it for a minute and I remember hoping he was right. Looking back he was absolutely right.

Maybe he should be a psychiatrist.

When you're holding your child, all of the things you were worried about either melt away or become unimportant. It's difficult to describe but you'll understand when it happens. Trust me and try to relax a little. Seriously. Take a deep breath and then a sedative of your choosing, just for good measure.

The truth is, the anxiety leading up to having a child is *way* worse than the anxiety of actually having the child. Think of it as jumping out of an airplane. It's tough to strap on the parachute and take that first step, but once you're in a free fall hurtling back toward the earth at 120 mph, worrying at that stage seems kind of pointless. All you can do at that point is pull the rip cord, let the wind take you, and hope you remembered where the telephone poles were.

3

Getting Pregnant (Not You, Obviously)

Eventually after many, many "discussions" my wife and I were off to the races. We agreed it was time to get pregnant. Now when I say "agreed," I really mean that my wife was ready and I had run out of excuses to wait. "We're too young," "Wait until we have a house," "I want to see Paris," "I want to buy a submarine . . ." But we weren't getting any younger and it was definitely time to let the genie out of the bottle. Of course, just because the decision was made didn't mean I felt any better about it.

This is where I have to give my wife a lot of credit. She knew I was not necessarily handling the "we've decided to get pregnant" thing very well. We were out doing errands one day and she was acting strangely. She had to get a baby shower gift for one of her friends. We pulled into the immense parking lot of Babies "R" Us and she unhesitantly asked if I wanted to wait in the car. I had never been in a Babies "R" Us and God bless her, she knew it wouldn't help me want to have a child. She was really pushing for me to stay in the car. But I said no, I would go in with her. See? I can be supportive.

Let's just say she was right on the money. Babies "R" Us is a horrible, horrible store. From the moment the automatic doors slide open it feels like you've just entered into the carnival from Ray Bradbury's *Something Wicked This Way Comes*. You are assaulted with all kinds of sights, smells, and feelings of subtle, off-putting dread. Instead of evil clowns and carnival barkers you get screaming kids, yelling pregnant women, and employees, who instead of helping you really just want to hang themselves. Honestly, the only telltale difference between the evil carnival and Babies "R" Us is greasepaint, a top hat, and an evil-sounding calliope. Actually, we registered for an evil-sounding calliope, so that doesn't count.

I then noticed that my wife kind of had the same stunned expression on her face as I did. Then I realized *nobody* wants to go to a Babies "R" Us. Some stores just exist because as big of a hassle as they are, they are still the only game in town. Want cheap baby crap on a Sunday? Gotta go to the BRU. It's like Blockbuster was before Netflix came along and gave them a nice, well-deserved ass kicking.

The trip to Babies "R" Us reminded me that the recurring thing for men—or at least for me, anyway—was that the anxiety and worry were always worse than the actual event. Once we decided to get pregnant, it was like a weight was lifted off my chest . . . for about two seconds. It was replaced with a much larger and heavier weight, but still, everything is a stage. Dread one stage; it happens—then on to dreading the next one. But the good news is that eventually the dread gets smaller and smaller until it settles into a comfortable feeling of constant annoyance. But really, isn't that how we feel all the time anyway? So after some time you'll be joyfully back to the beginning. Circle of Life.

There are a few useful things I've learned in the getting-pregnant process. The first thing you have to take into consideration about getting pregnant is a woman's biological clock. It's not a figment of their imaginations. Oh, it's real. Believe me. Sure, you hear it ticking, but when my wife hit her midthirties I swear her biological clock had gone digital and was attached to a car alarm. It's like a switch goes off in women. There's no other way to describe it. My wife went from wanting a baby, to wanting a baby *now*. It was as if she were saying "I want a baby *right now*. No, I want one yesterday. Just invent a time machine. What's taking so long?"

God help us if women figure out a way to have babies

without gestation and labor. Because the experience is so horrible (for both of you) that it slows things down if they ever want another one. Trust me, after the *magic* of pregnancy and childbirth, my wife, who originally wanted 3–4 kids, was now down to 1–2. Score one for nature. Every once in a while my wife will have a friend who tells her she loves being pregnant. We both call those women "crazy." I am reminded of Bill Murray as the dental patient who refuses novocaine while Steve Martin works on him in *Little Shop of Horrors*. Of course, you could count Jack Nicholson too in the original Roger Corman movie. Think I forgot? Anyway, the point is, it takes all kinds.

Now in her midthirties, my wife wanted to be pregnant *now*. Did I mention that? She made that abundantly clear. One day I tried to explain to her that the phrase "I'm ovulating. Now come over here, shut up, and do your job" is *not* a turn-on. Then again, it kinda is.

The good news is you can sit back, relax, and enjoy some unusually motivated and enthusiastic sex. You can even make a few, um, "requests," until your wife figures out you're trying to exploit the situation and calls you on it. Thankfully, after that happened she kept the black leather armor and elf ears on anyway. She's a sport. Bad dark elf. Bad.

Mythological fantasies aside, after a few months my wife was not getting pregnant. Mainly because I was faking it. Ha, just kidding. You know we can't fake it. Contrary to what your wife may say at this point, it is perfectly normal to not get pregnant right away. Now your wife will star in her own game show: *The Not Getting Pregnant Blame Game.* Guess who always "wins" the first round? Yes, that's right, the one with the penis.

My wife's first explanation for the trouble getting pregnant was that there was something wrong with me and my sperm. Whenever there's a problem with anything, women always blame our genitals. Granted, a lot of the time they're right to do so, but not this time. We talked about the first step to finding the problem, which is checking for fertility. She wanted me checked first, obviously. Remember, penis = blame. But I knew I would be fine. I not only was sure my boys could swim, but they have also had plenty of practice at this point on both away and home games, if you know what I mean.

Oh, but the bonus round: In addition to her not getting pregnant right away, I was still on Zoloft at this point. And Zoloft has a bit of a side effect. Decreased sex drive and delayed ejaculation. I could not have picked two things to make my wife angrier. She accused me of doing it on purpose. Like I had secret meetings in a seedy bar with a Pfizer sales rep. "Okay, it's between you guys and Rogaine. Which will make me orgasm less?" So now the sex went from enthusiastic to time consuming and annoying. For her.

But we soon found the real culprit in our not-getting-pregnant saga. And for once the blame could not be put on my genitals. And the winner is . . . the Ovulation Cycle! Apparently women only ovulate for a short time each month. This is not something we men know, or should even be expected to know. Supposedly women are in tune with their bodies and know when this whole magical *Ring of the Nibelung* takes place every month.

When taking the ovulation cycle into account, sex became a game of timing. Enthusiastic sex on ovulation days, and "don't touch me" on the off days, as I was supposed to be "saving it up" for the next ovulation round. She also told me not to masturbate for the same reason. I tried to explain to her that there was "plenty to go around" but she didn't find that at all amusing. So we stuck to our schedule and I masturbated when she was out of the house or asleep, the way I always did. At some point the sex got so routine that I started describing it as "our duty to the Party." But like I said, at least at first the sex was definitely enthusiastic, which was "doubleplusgood"! Cool! There's no sex like Orwellian sex.

Ah, but the plot thickened. The ironic thing was that my wife did *not* know when she was ovulating. She thought she did but she was off by a few days. That's all it takes to screw up the timing. It has to be pretty exact. There's no win, place, or show in the ovulation race. Now, how did she find this out, you may ask? Because of that two-faced bastard: science. Let me just say right now that science is not to be trusted. Sure, Thermoses and video games are great, but men never count on the dreaded ovulation kit. She bought one. She used it. It gave her results and told her *exactly* when she was ovulating. For reals. A few days later we had rigidly scheduled but newly enthusiastic ovulation sex. It's like Orwellian sex but with a dash of Joseph Heller irony.

With the help of the ovulation kit, after one college try my wife was pregnant. And so the journey began. That's all it took. A little bit of buttinsky help from our old pal science. But not all women are aware of ovulation kits. Unfortunately you can only suppress that information for so long. They'll find out about them, believe me. Even without Google. She'll have some loudmouth friend at work who will tell her *all* about them. Claim ignorance. One thing I noticed about wives is that if you fake ignorance, they usually believe you. Most of the time they assume we're not faking and that we're just constantly ignorant.

The way you'll get pregnant will be as personal to you as your own child will be. It may happen right away, maybe in a few months, or you may need some help from that fair weather friend, science. However it happens, you will now be "off to see the Wizard" and have started making your very own Munchkin. As long as it's not a flying monkey, you should be all right. Then again, how cool would that be?

DANTE ALIGHIERI'S NINE INFERNAL CIRCLES OF BABIES "R" US

**1ST CIRCLE:
LIMBO**
▼

The unease you get while driving to the store.

**2ND CIRCLE:
THE LUSTFUL**
▼

The reason you're driving to Babies "R" Us in the first place.

**3RD CIRCLE:
THE GLUTTONOUS**
▼

Looking up someone's stupid baby registry and
it has like a hundred things on it.

**4TH CIRCLE:
THE AVARICIOUS AND THE PRODIGALS**
▼

Let's face it, if you were rich you wouldn't be going to Babies "R" Us.

**5TH CIRCLE:
THE WRATHFUL AND SULLEN**
▼

Husbands.

**6TH CIRCLE:
THE HERETICS**
▼

Someone who is at the store and says, "We can get most of
this crap cheaper online. Why are we even here?"

**7TH CIRCLE:
THE VIOLENT**
▼

Never go when Babies "R" Us is having a sale.

**8TH CIRCLE:
FRAUD**
▼

New and improved! Some assembly required! Now in stock!
Yeah, sure.

**9TH CIRCLE:
TREACHERY**
▼

The return desk.

The Pregnancy, or: How I Learned to Stop Worrying and Love the Bomb . . . er, Baby

At the beginning of my wife's pregnancy I felt this weird mixture of anxiety, dread, guilt, and fear. *Now I've gone and done it* was all I kept thinking. Like Wally and the Beaver had spilled milk all over the kitchen floor. And then Wally killed a hooker and hid her body in the Nevada desert. Sometimes my anxiety makes me overly creative. Having a child is scary enough, but in our initial fear we men forget about something very important: getting through the next nine months. It's like the calm before the—no, wait, it's like the storm before the storm.

So what to expect during the pregnancy? The problem is we men have absolutely no freaking idea. Up until now the only real contact we have *ever* had with pregnant women is in the movies or if one of our friends' wives gets pregnant. But basically we try to avoid them. Really, there's nothing there for us, so why bother?

Unfortunately, that puts us at a distinct disadvantage when it happens to us. I just kept saying over and over, "My wife is pregnant. *My* wife." This was happening right in my own house! Like most men, I had no idea what to do when confronted with a pregnant woman. OK, maybe "confronted" is the wrong word. Actually, I just looked it up: *to oppose (something hostile or dangerous) with firmness or courage.* So yes, confronted is right on the money. The first thing I tried to do was not panic. Then I panicked. Everything I had ever heard in passing about pregnant women was now coming to mind. How big was she going to get? Exactly how bad would the mood swings be? Wasn't there something I should know about water breaking, and how can you break water? What was it Kevin Bacon said in *She's Having a Baby*? "We're gonna need a bigger boat." No, that's not it. Dammit!

When I looked at my pregnant wife, I not only saw

the woman I loved, but now she was also a familial time bomb with a little nine-month readout on her belly. As her stomach grew, it was like the countdown numbers got bigger and brighter until she was ready to blow. All I could think was, *Man, in nine months that sucker is gonna drop*. Kind of like the Times Square New Year's Eve ball getting ready to shoot out of her uterus. Only, with more fireworks.

But first things first. The immediate question we have is: Can I have sex with my wife while she's pregnant? The answer is yes, up until labor, if you can believe that. I mean, at this point the damage has been done. Go for it. You certainly can't get her more pregnant. Just know that it's not going to be pretty. My wife started feeling very self-conscious the moment she started showing. She began to feel "less attractive" and I had to reassure her that wasn't the case. You're going to need to be supportive. Granted, that's not our strong suit as men, but your wife will appreciate the effort. Thankfully men are not encumbered with this "feeling less attractive" response, ever. Then again, maybe we should be. It might stop overweight French Canadian men from wearing thongs on the beach.

The reality is that as the belly gets bigger, sex gets more awkward and more of an emotional minefield. There's now a mix of anxiety, fear, hormones, and a sprinkling of depression all in bed with you. It's like you're having a threesome with a sober Judy Garland. The bottom line is that when you get closer to the birth, don't be surprised to see sobbing and crying in the middle of sex. My wife hated when I did that.

Also, as a weird side effect involving the mail, once my wife was pregnant she immediately stopped getting Victoria's Secret catalogs. It's like they *know* somehow. Previously, my wife was getting about three or four *a day*. I swear, they must have their own mailmen who secretly watch for a car seat being installed or a crib being delivered. An alarm then goes off in the subscription department, and someone declares, "They won't be needing this anymore." I ended up having to steal my neighbor's copy.

So what happens during this trip down the big pregnant rabbit hole? Let's break it down into the three stages of pregnancy: the Trimesters. Or as I refer to them: Moe, Larry, and Curly.

The First Trimester (Moe):

It began with my wife throwing up one morning. Since we hadn't eaten at Sizzler the night before, we thought it was time for the pregnancy test. She took the test. She was pregnant. Then I threw up. Oh, my God, this was it! It was really happening! Sometimes there are false positives, but don't get your hopes up. The doctor will determine for sure, but chances are that blue line or cross is accurate and will be burned into your brain for the rest of your life.

At this point my wife was incredibly happy, and I had a blank dumb look on my face. It was too much to process and I had already shut down. Unfortunately, my wife noticed. I received a flurry of questions with no real expectation of having them answered: "What's wrong with you? Why aren't you more excited? You should be happy! WHY AREN'T YOU HAPPY!?!?!"

My wife's shrill emotional voice snapped me out of my shocked stupor. Unfortunately I had no idea where I was or what was going on. But through the haze I knew I had to watch my step and choose my next words carefully. Let's just say I didn't. I stammered something like, "I *am* happy" quite unconvincingly and not even really all that coherently. I got the stink eye. Both eyes. Then there was an uncomfortable silence that lasted for about twenty-nine hours. I used that time to finish *Half-Life 2*.

What women don't realize is that it takes us men a long time to adjust to anything. When we got a cat, I was freaked out for a while. I was afraid it would scratch my face off as soon as I was asleep. But eventually I calmed down and everything was fine. I still don't like the way the cat looks at me sometimes, but that's another story. I got used to the cat, but it took time. Heck, Archie Bunker didn't like it when someone else sat in his chair. We just don't like change. So a baby? That's the granddaddy of all changes. We need lots of time to get used to it. Why do you think the gestation period for humans is nine months? To develop and grow a fetus? No. It's because that's the minimum amount of time men need to get used to the idea of having a child. Explain to your wife you *are* happy and that it's a big, life-changing adjustment and you just need some time to get used to it. If you phrase your lie logically like that, then it will be harder for her to argue with you. Harder, but not impossible.

But cheer up and don't worry because eventually you'll come around and adjust. Trust me. It's just going to take some time. My wife even started cutting me some slack and actually acknowledged that I was handling it pretty well. So in other words, it was her turn to lie. And that's fine. The point is you're lying to each other to make the other one feel better. Isn't that what being parents is all about?

However, keep in mind miscarriages do occur, and they are tragic. They usually happen during the first trimester. As a rule, it's good not to tell anyone you're pregnant until the second trimester. Immediate family should be the only exception. If you tell people too early and a miscarriage does occur, all the outpouring of sympathy will just make you and your wife feel worse. Of course, just know that your wife may ignore this advice and tell every single person she knows immediately, from her parents to a guy standing in line with her at the car wash. So if you are at your local grocery store one day and the checker gives you a knowing look, you'll know your wife has been there within the last twelve hours.

If everything goes well, this first trimester is an interesting time. Every woman is different. You hear that a lot. But really, are they? They're all moody, hungry, happy, and sad, in any order or combination. One from Column A and two from Column B. Plus a side of hot-and-sour soup.

In addition to mood swings and perceived mental illness, there will be actual physical illness as well. My wife threw up all the time. Morning sickness? Not just for mornings anymore. At one point I just started sleeping wrapped in plastic. It made cleanup easier. One night my wife ate some watermelon, and I felt like I was sleeping at a Gallagher concert.

But it didn't stop there. Sometimes my wife would throw up and then eat a huge meal like some moody reverse bulimic. Best not to point that out, though. In retrospect, I probably should've kept that to myself. In fact, the best advice for a pregnancy will always be to *just stay out of the way and keep your mouth shut*. This advice will be repeated over and over until it sinks in.

To balance out the throwing up and other pregnancy "side effects" is the glow. It's an interesting phenomenon.

The pregnancy glow says many things, like, "I am so happy I'm pregnant. I can't wait to start a family. This is the happiest I've ever been. When I'm hungry, you better get me EXACTLY what I want." Learn to read the glow. But the glow will always start from one place. The belly. When my wife was pregnant, the belly was the center of the universe. She would rub it, talk to it, and warned me that if I ever went through with my threat of drawing a big giant happy face on it in Magic Marker while she was asleep, I would be in trouble. I believed her.

During this first trimester the belly begins to get bigger but not too terribly big. But it is growing every day. And it's watching. Especially when you sleep, the belly watches. Always watching you, sort of like the damn cat. OK, maybe I was just being paranoid. But one night, when I couldn't sleep, I was looking at the belly and in the back of my head I could swear I heard Moe say, "Oh, a wise guy. Spread out . . ."

The Second Trimester (Larry):

To the day, my wife stopped throwing up. She felt better. She was enjoying her pregnancy. She wasn't at all moody or unpredictable. One of those statements is false. Look, let's get this out of the way. You're going to get yelled at. Sorry. It's not personal; it's hormonal. My wife and I once got into a fight because she bent down to get something in front of her.

"It hurts me to bend down!"

"Then why didn't you ask me to get it for you?"

That was it. It was on. Never, EVER use logic on a pregnant woman. I'm telling you right now: Just shut up and take it. It's not your fault. OK, well, it's kind of your fault, but the mistake most men make is not understanding what's going on inside a pregnant woman's body. Granted, none of us really understands, but the process must be respected. So understand that you'll . . . never understand. Getting angry at your pregnant wife for being moody and yelling at you is like getting mad at the puppy for peeing on the rug. It's in their nature and they can't help it. There is nothing you can do to prevent or avoid it, so just accept it. Look, your wife gets it. After the hormones have leveled off for the evening, sit down and enjoy some quiet time together. Eat some ice cream or chocolate, if there's any left, and then relax and watch some nice, hard-core pornography.

One of the things we argued about was feeling the baby kick. During the second trimester a pregnant woman will feel the baby kick. That's not the problem. The problem is she'll want *you* to feel it. Now, I didn't want to feel the baby kick. I've just seen too many science fiction movies to be comfortable with it. This was taken as a personal insult by my wife and not as part of my normal psychosis, as it should have been. It would have taken too long to explain, so I forced myself to put my hands on her alien cocoon. Then I couldn't feel anything, which was apparently my fault.

"You're not even trying!"

"How am *I* not even trying?"

After a few more attempts at mind-melding with my wife's stomach, I finally did feel the slightest of vibrations. It was almost like Morse code. I think it was saying, "Move along, folks. Show's over."

Two shows nightly in the belly aside, sometimes your wife may have weeks without a mood swing or an outrageous demand. This is incredibly disconcerting because you begin to wonder if she's leading up to something. Like she's saving it up. Is it all going to come out at once? Finally, while you are watching your *Babylon 5* DVDs, will she just explode? "You did this to me, I'm hungry, I can't believe how big I am, my mother was right about you, and so was your mother, why do you keep watching that stupid show? It went off the air years ago . . ."

Mood swings are just one of the many changes that are going on inside and outside a woman's body at this time. You never really know what to expect. Sure, the belly's bigger, but there could be unexpected hitchhikers like acne, rashes, and even blurry vision. My wife had these weird symmetrical red slashes on her ass. It looked like she . . . sat on an angry wolverine. Now, I hope that made you laugh because I'm going to get it once she reads this.

With all the physical changes comes discomfort. My wife was pretty big at this point. She was sleeping on her back and sometimes on her side but would frequently wake up in the middle of the night because she was uncomfortable. She also was starting to complain of back pain. This is usually where men think, "Well, she can't get any bigger," and we're always wrong.

The one bonus is that her breasts will be bigger. Just make sure you avoid any discussions of "were they too small before?" because it's a trap. During this trimester a woman's breasts are sensitive and bloated, but they are bigger. And as long as they're bigger, guys don't really give a shit about anything else. I think that is intentional. Bigger breasts on a pregnant woman are nature's consolation prize for the man. Enjoy your gift because your wife probably isn't. As I was . . . admiring . . . my wife's new breasts, I suddenly heard a bunch of slapping sounds and then I heard Larry say, "Hey, leave 'em alone!"

The Third Trimester (Curly):

Oh, man, my wife was huge at this point. She wasn't sleeping well, which means *I* wasn't sleeping well. We would have many late night "discussions" about what was coming, mainly because she couldn't sleep. We discussed everything from our nervousness about the birth and our new monthly budget to if the new *Harry Potter* movies would be any good. "Not if Chris Columbus is involved" would always be my response. For everything.

The thing is, this is supposed to be the happiest time for you both, and yet no one is really happy. During this trimester there were still a million things to do, like figure out the @#*)& car seat with more tethers than an octopus and filling out all the hospital preregistration paperwork, which I swear came straight from the movie *Brazil*. Which, FYI, I think they toss because when you get to the hospital, you will be filling it all out again anyway. The thrill of the pregnancy was over, for all three of us. It was a tense and uncomfortable time. Let me just add that if there was ever a time to keep your mouth shut about things, now's the time. (I told you that advice would be repeated. Has it sunk in yet?) Just nod, smile, and make sure there is always gas in the car.

At this point my wife's love of being pregnant had faded and turned into "I want this thing out of me." But no matter what I said to comfort her, like, "It will be over soon" to, "I just keep thinking of John Hurt in *Alien*" it was met with shock and awe. Of course, if you've had enough and you want to induce labor early, you could just come home one day and say something like, "Great news! I just bought a motorcycle!" or, "I just quit my job!"

When things get tense, and they will, just remember that these are the last three months, which will both relieve and horrify you at the same time. Tick tick tick tick . . . You can now almost see Ryan Seacrest in Times Square getting ready to start counting. Ten . . . nine . . . eight . . .

But take heart. Like *American Idol*, those excruciating last few weeks were soon over. Even though everything was coming to a head, including the nervousness, anxiety, and the sudden renewed collegiate level interest in Jell-O shooters, we knew showtime was right around the corner. Then in my head I heard Curly say, "Moe, Larry, the Cheese!" for absolutely no reason whatsoever.

THINGS TO NEVER SAY TO A PREGNANT WOMAN

1. Wow, you're gaining weight like a motherfucker.
2. Why don't you get it yourself?
3. Well, um, do *you* think you look pretty?
4. Are you going to finish that?
5. Angelina Jolie didn't gain weight during her pregnancy because she had a staff to do it for her. (Actually, that one you *can* say.)
6. Why have you stopped wearing makeup?

7. Don't you have anything other than sweatpants?
8. Are you sure you want to have a baby?
9. Are you sure it's mine?
10. Can you stop yelling at me long enough to at least give me a hand job?

Homework I Really Don't Feel Like Doing: Classes, Movies, and Books

The first thing I noticed about all the "prep" work on having a child is that there is an entire industry dependent on the fact that you and your wife are nervous and anxious about reproducing. From the latest book to the newest car seat, "If you don't buy our shit, you're a bad parent!" You know that slogan is in some internal corporate memo somewhere deep in the bowels of Gerber, Graco, or Fisher-Price.

Let's take a look at classes first. There are a million

available to prepare you for having a child. Well, there are a million that scratch the surface of preparing you to have a child. Act now and you can learn everything from learning how to breathe and how to change diapers to something actually useful like what to do if your infant is choking. Learn new words like "swaddle," "hind milk," and "hospital co-pay."

When I first entered the class we were taking, I saw there was a doll in front of every couple. Yes, a doll. It's the only place in your life where you will be in a room full of dolls and no children. Unless you're in a Japanese horror movie. Or if you go to one of those creepy doll museums but really, what are the chances of that, unless your wife *really* hates you?

So we're sitting there waiting for class to start and I don't need to tell you I didn't want to be there. So the next thing that happened was really my wife's fault. I mean, you put a doll in front of me with a bunch of other nervous couples, what did she *think* was going to happen? Apparently you're not supposed to play with the doll and make it wave, mime going up the stairs, or pretend it's a ventriloquist dummy. Sometimes other expectant couples have no sense of humor.

The one thing we all seemed to have in common at these classes is that everyone is nervous, including the women. It's new territory for everyone. I noticed that the pregnant women mask their nervousness with their pregnant happy glow, and men mask it with their look of complete boredom as the instructor at the head of the class drones on and on forever about things we don't want to know. But still, despite all that happy boredom there is that undercurrent of "Oh, my God, I better pay attention or my child will never survive." Market forces at work.

It was basically an "intro" class so we learned the basics, like diapering and feeding. We each took a turn with the doll but by that time I wasn't really allowed anywhere near it. I think I was the first person attending that class to ever get a detention. Needless to say, I was bored and just kept watching the clock and occasionally glanced at the annoyed look on my wife's face.

Then the instructor turned the lights off. Mind-numbing boredom suddenly and unexpectedly turned into mind-numbing horror. I was not prepared for what followed. They showed a movie. Not a good movie by any stretch of the imagination. Let's just say two thumbs *way* down. For the love of God, it was worse than anything shown in driver's ed. This horror fest showed a close-up of a woman giving birth! Not that fake uncomfortable insert shot in *Knocked Up*, but the real thing. Oh, my God, I don't want to see my own wife doing this. Now I'm going to watch some fat stranger do it on film? I swear, it was like if Stephen King made a porno. Like *Debbie Does Carrie*. It resembled one of those scary movies that frighten you into not committing crimes or driving drunk. But they show that childbirth movie *way* too late in the process. Show that film to someone right *before* they decide to have a kid and see what happens. In a hundred years China would have four people living in it.

And while we're at it, what kind of crazy exhibitionist woman says, "No, honey, our video camera is not enough. I want everyone to see this! I want a full crew in here, a good lighting package, and see if you can get an HD camera."

As the horror continued to unfold, my wife noticed I had become a bit pale at that point. I then noticed that she too looked nervous and uncomfortable. Really? I can't imagine why. I'm no expert, but footage of a strange woman screaming at the top of her lungs while giving birth is probably not the best way to reassure nervous pregnant women about childbirth. My wife then leaned over and whispered in my ear, "I want a C-section." I totally empathized as the horror on screen continued. And as far as the men go, most of us were already setting some room aside in the "repressed memory" section of our brains before the end credits even rolled.

It was as if the reality of what was to come was not only setting in, but shown to us on a large screen. And we paid good money for this?! It would have been easier and cheaper to just pay a homeless person to hit us with a wine bottle. No one said anything for a while after that film was done. Everyone was shocked into silence. The balance of the lecture could have been delivered by a circus clown and no one would have noticed or said anything. The rest of the class was a surreal blur about water breaking and C-sections and maybe even unicorns for all I remember. The movie had temporarily paralyzed both my short- and long-term memory. Even my wife commented that the film was . . . "unnecessary."

There are so many classes too. Although thankfully not too many more with movies. But it's like they never freaking end. What a racket! There are intro classes. Then classes for breathing (Lamaze) and childbirthing. Infant CPR! Wait, OK, that one's important. That one we did go to and it was the most practical of all of them. But there are also classes on nutrition, labor, finances, seat belts, safety, babyproofing, preparing your child for *Are You Smarter than a 5th Grader*, etc. There's even a class about how to hypnotize your wife so she can't feel the childbirth pain. Please, if I were able to hypnotize my wife, it would not be to prevent her feeling pain. "OK, now when I snap my fingers, you're going to wake up and be OK with having a threesome. Then you're going to act like a chicken." But I digress.

Finally I just got fed up with all the freaking classes. At some point I just went, "That's it! No more classes.

I'm only going to the ones that can ultimately save my child's life because I have no idea what I'm doing." So in other words, pick infant choking/CPR classes and pretty much treat the rest as optional or corporate marketing ploys.

The good thing is once the baby is born, you won't have the time or energy to go to any classes for a very long time. You've graduated, and the on-the-job training begins. However, this time there is no diploma and you don't get a senior week. But there will still be a lot of late nights, crying, and throwing up, so in a way it's similar.

All Those Parenting Books

Man, there are so many now. And I already checked—not one graphic novel. You wonder where you should even begin. But how do you pick which ones are good and which ones are crap? You and your wife want some books, dammit, but which ones? You want something helpful, or celebrity-driven tripe? There are even fewer choices on the fatherhood side. And the stuff that is there is, well . . . let's just say good luck getting through one. I was so bored reading one that I might as well have been reading a Nathaniel Hawthorne novel.

The point is, there are hundreds of books out there.

Most of them give the same info repackaged or they just give you bad advice. It's like every time Britney Spears goes into rehab, another parenting book gets its wings. For sanity and simplicity, I recommend going old school. Hey, sometimes the classics are still the best. *Dr. Spock* really is the *Lawrence of Arabia* of parenting books. Go with Dr. Spock as your primary reference book. There's a reason he's sold more than 50 million copies. That's pretty good for a book that isn't about a wizard named Harry. Now you've got your foundation. Then pick up any other book you or your wife wants. At worst, when you have company over, they'll think you're being responsible when they see the stack of baby books on the table. They don't need to know they haven't been opened. And they make great drink coasters.

What to Expect When You're Expecting is a great book . . . FOR YOUR WIFE. Do not even look at it unless you want to get angry or have a very ironic laugh, like when that stupid loud guy at work makes a horrible joke. He thinks you're laughing *with* him. *What to Expect When You're Expecting* has a very small chapter for the fathers called "Fathers Are Expectant, Too." I'm sure some genius editor told the authors they could reach more people, maybe even some MEN if they added a chapter about men during the pregnancy. After reading the chapter I looked immediately at the names of the authors. Yep. Heidi, Arlene, and Sandee. Well, ladies, let's just say your "father" chapter is incredibly off base and pretty much borders on the absurd. It reads like "This is what men are thinking, if they were women."

It's no surprise that most of the "advice" these three ladies give to fathers centers around being supportive and understanding of the woman. I began to wonder if the authors had even talked to a man ever in their lives or even cared what they had to say. My favorite line was "I find my wife incredibly sexy now. But she hasn't been in the mood." The explanation—wait, I had to keep checking back because I couldn't believe it—" . . . many men find the roundness and fullness of the pregnant form surprisingly sensual, even erotic." First of all, no man outside of a mental institution would say this, ever. Here's my question: "If you're so attracted to her now, how repulsive did you find your wife's body before she got pregnant?" It's beyond ridiculous. Over 10 million copies in print! Please, as a request for future editions, just take out that chapter. Seriously.

As my wife and I were looking for books to read, we also noticed there were a lot of "trend" books with astonishingly large marketing budgets. Do you want to learn all about infant massage, attachment parenting, Baby Yoga (Baby Yoda would be interesting, though), and the new diaperless babies? I'm just kidding. Of course you don't.

But your wife might, so make sure you hide those books. You'll thank me later.

So I've come down hard on the baby book industry. And yes, I am well aware of the enormous irony. But I stand by my assertion that for real, time-tested, and practical advice you should stick to the classics like those written by Dr. Spock.

But even if you do manage to actually read a few of these books, keep in mind child care is not an exact science. No book is completely accurate or should be followed to the letter. Ever. One of the things my wife and I learned, the hard way, as you often do, is that you should treat every piece of baby advice either read or heard as a guideline and not an absolute. And Dr. Spock agrees with me. OK, maybe I just agree with him, but let's not split hairs. After a few nights of trying various book advice, friend advice, and family advice for burping, crying, and sleeping, we realized our baby was unique (as yours will be) and sometimes the advice worked and sometimes it just made things worse. Your baby will tell you what works and what doesn't, very loudly. Listen to him first before you listen to anyone else.

Here's one last piece of advice. Please keep in mind you have to do as much of your "book learnin'" as you can *before* the baby is born. Because after the baby is born you won't have the time or energy to read anything longer than a delivery menu.

HOW DR. SPOCK IS JUST LIKE MR. SPOCK

Dr. Spock	Mr. Spock
Dr. Spock was an enterprising doctor and navy officer who changed the science of child care.	Mr. Spock was the science officer of the USS *Enterprise*.
Dr. Spock is great in a pinch to soothe the nerves of a semiconscious new parent.	Mr. Spock has a great Vulcan nerve pinch to soothe his enemies into unconsciousness.
Dr. Spock is a parent's most trusted advisor and his help is critical at the genesis of your new life.	Mr. Spock was brought back to life with the critical help of Captain Kirk using the Genesis Device.
Dr. Spock wrote his book because too much baby advice can meld together in your mind and give you a whale of a headache.	Mr. Spock once mind-melded with a whale in *The Voyage Home*.
Dr. Spock makes a point that ear infections are a common trouble in young children and are often caused by a blocked eustachian tube.	Mr. Spock has pointed ears and removed a block caused by tribbles in a Space Station 7 tube.

6

Health and Tests You Can't Study For

"I'll take the number one concern for expecting parents please, Alex."
"What is: What if my baby isn't healthy?"

With pregnancy, there is always a risk. And the longer you wait to have a child, the higher the risk gets. Not only is it harder to get pregnant, but there is a greater risk of prenatal complications. Or so our doctor kept telling us. It wasn't really helpful information, to be honest. And not something we didn't already know. Everyone from your parents to the guy selling you weed tells you not to wait too long to have kids. The last thing a scared pregnant couple needs is a lecture. But our ob-gyn is the one who knows how to work all of that ultrasound equipment so we just smiled and let him have his say. Well, that's not true. We didn't really smile.

Age is where it's pretty much the woman's show. My wife got pregnant in her midthirties, which according to our judgmental doctor, was late. Like we had gone up to Mother Nature and slapped her in the face. And then tried to fool her with some type of butter substitute.

Our doctor continued his age tirade and said that by age forty half of a woman's eggs are bad. Yes, but which half? No response. All right then. In fact, because my wife was pregnant and over the terribly old age of thirty-five she needed all of these other tests. As unfair as this is, for women, it is the truth. Men's sperm generally stays good, and we go through it at a sometimes alarming rate. Age doesn't matter as much for us as it does for women. There are still risks for older men but we can always pull a Tony Randall. But women without the help of biology-altering fertility drugs are indeed on a clock.

The health of your child begins with you and your wife, but mostly falls on your wife's health. Is she overweight? Does she exercise? How's her cholesterol? Does she consider tobacco a vegetable? Simply put, a healthy woman increases the chances of having a healthy baby, especially if you're having a child a little later in your mid to late thirties. Of course, even though you're not carrying the child yourself, it wouldn't hurt to put down the Krispy Kreme and go to the gym every once in a while. Try to be healthier. It's a good thing to do even if you're not having a child. Stop eating so many processed foods and try an apple periodically. Plus, getting in better shape will help you both have more energy once the baby is here. You're going to need it.

Will it guarantee a healthy baby? Of course not. Nothing in life is guaranteed. Except maybe that Keanu Reeves will never win an Oscar. The good news is that there are plenty of tests available throughout the process to see if your baby is healthy. Some people are against all of the tests during pregnancy. Screw that. Get every test imaginable. We did. You want to be sure as you can about everything? Get poked, prodded, and examined as much as your insurance company allows. And if that test you want isn't covered, then keep the credit card handy.

Obviously, everyone wants a completely healthy child. It's what we all wish and pray for. But the reality is that no kid is completely healthy. Sorry to burst your bubble. Chances are he or she will have some kind of allergy/asthma/colic, get chronic ear infections, or think Larry the Cable Guy is funny. Something will go wrong.

It's normal and not your fault. If your baby is completely healthy with not one problem, and as he gets older he just never seems to get sick, then you should probably start checking his body for a few sixes. You know, the mark. And good luck.

Like College Parties, Sex Is a 50-50 Chance

I remember really, really wishing our baby was going to be a boy. I was thinking, well, if I'm going to have a child, please let it be a boy. Fifty-fifty chance, right? Maybe, just maybe, I had willed that Y chromosome into her egg with the sheer power of my mind. Like I had done the Jedi mind trick on all the sperm with the Xs. "This is not the egg you're looking for . . ."

Most men want a boy. I certainly did. There are many reasons for this. One of them is to continue the family name. An heir to the throne, if you will. The other reason is that we want at least one person in the house we kind of understand. Even if all they do is scream, sleep, and poop. Now, that we can understand. We know a lot more about baseball mitts than dollhouses. G.I. Joe vs. Barbie. In this whole baby pre-show we men search for one little piece of comfort or normality. Something we can grasp and get a handle on. The idea of . . . maleness. Let's face it, we know nothing about women. We really don't. How we get any of them to marry us is a mystery. Oh, wait, that's usually their idea. Again, another book.

So did I get a boy? No—no, I didn't. One fine day the sonogram revealed our child was simply not going to grow a penis. It was a little baby girl and my wife was overjoyed. Was it a disappointment to me when I found out we were having a girl? At first, yes. I was very disappointed. I mean, way beyond *Star Wars* prequels and Kirk falling off a scaffolding and dying in *Star Trek: Generations* disappointed. Really, really disappointed.

My wife couldn't understand why I was so upset. Of course she couldn't. *She* was getting a girl. I felt like the Soup Nazi from *Seinfeld* was telling me to get out of his store and yelling, "No boy for you!"

But those feelings of . . . buyer's remorse faded. They really did. As my wife's belly got bigger, I got more used to the idea of having a girl. I didn't bring it up again because my wife was just getting angrier every time I mentioned it. Well, she was pregnant at the time so I'll give her some slack. But the disappointment didn't really *fully* go away until I met her. My child, not my wife. Not that there was any disappointment in meeting my wife. I'm going to stop typing now.

Well, that certainly made naming our child a bit easier. Cut the possible names down by about half. My wife wanted the name Isabella. I wanted to look through all the baby name books, and I did. When I was done, we named our daughter Isabella.

I learned there are some real upsides to having a girl. Daughters tend to be close with their fathers, especially when they get older. "Daddy's little girl." That means you always get to be the good cop. Until she starts dating, of course. Then you just have to be the cop.

Now, if you are having a boy, congrats. You already have a leg up. You were a boy once, so you have a few experiences and a frame of reference to draw upon. Until you find out having your own child is completely different from interacting with any other child you've had contact with up until now. But at least you'll be able to play with cooler toys. Pirate ships are more fun than tea parties. Of course, you could always try to sneak a pirate into your daughter's tea party, to see if she's paying attention.

We had some pregnant friends who didn't want to know the sex of their child before the birth. They wanted it to be a surprise. I, however, felt I had had enough surprises. I wanted as many variables eliminated as possible. It gave me a nice false sense of having control over something. Men like false senses of anything. We're in our own little world and we like it there. We'll come in and visit reality periodically, but it's not where we live. Think of reality as a man's summer home.

I knew it would help me prepare mentally and emotionally if I knew who was coming to dinner. And I have to say it *did* help me. I really liked knowing I was going to have a girl ahead of time. But if you want to go all *Deer Hunter* and play a little prenatal Russian roulette, then be my guest. Of course, you're going to have to paint everything beige.

8

Getting Your House Ready for Your New Permanent Roommate

Oh, man, where to begin. I looked at my wife's pregnant stomach and then at the room our new baby was going to occupy. For some reason the movie *A Bridge Too Far* came to mind. There were a bazillion things to do, and would we get them all done in time?

The room had to be painted, the nursery "pattern" or "theme" had to be picked out, color schemes, sheets, furniture picked out and assembled, etc. But now here's the thing: If you're having a girl, like we were, you will have very little to do with any of these decisions. Remember when you got married and a lot of the decision making involving the wedding was done by your wife and her mom? Welcome to the flashback.

Don't get me wrong; you're going to have to do most of the work but you can shut off the old brain and let your wife do her thing. Let her pretend she's the host of one of those HGTV shows and watch her . . . cry havoc and let slip the dogs of baby design.

Personally, I say start *at least four months in advance* getting the room ready. Decisions about themes and color schemes that you couldn't care less about will nevertheless take a fair amount of time to come to fruition.

Now this is again where some trickery comes into play. Think of it as a hormonally driven game of baby room chicken. My wife pretended to be interested in my opinion because she thought I should feel involved in the baby room's interior design. My mistake was that I forgot to feign interest, which was my part in this tenuous, pastel-driven charade. She outplayed me and I got caught. As soon as those words left my mouth, I knew it was over. You know, the words "I don't care; you pick." She pounced on me like a cat on a mouse covered in gravy. "What's wrong with you? Don't you care about your child's room? Now come on and help me decide: Taffy Pink, Pink Sparkle, or Pink Lily?!" Ultimately, we went with purple.

But wait, there's more! Remember that sweet baby room furniture you saw in the store? Well, not only will it not be in stock, but it will take weeks to get to your home. Then, when it gets to your house, it will look *nothing* like what you saw in the store. More like a three-dimensional jigsaw puzzle. Absolutely nothing comes preassembled. Cribs, bassinets, strollers, swings, toys, etc., all come in flat boxes and they all need to be put together—by you and maybe one of your drunk friends. That's the only way you'll get someone to help you, by the way. Ply them with alcohol. Your new life is now sponsored by Corona and IKEA.

The other really important thing about furniture and screw jobs is that even if you're not going to put the furniture together as soon as it is delivered, you have to immediately check it out to make sure it's not damaged. Sometimes the manufacturers will actually send you the replacement parts directly to your house. Sometimes. Most of the time they just giggle and tell you to take it back to the store.

You want to deal with as little extra stuff as possible once the baby arrives. In a perfect world you'd just have to deal with keeping your new baby alive. And frankly, that's plenty.

In addition to "some assembly required" everything needs batteries. Even if you think it doesn't, it does.

Swing? Batteries. Play mat? Batteries. Plush toy? Batteries. A book? Yes, a freaking book—batteries. These days *everything* lights up, talks, or vibrates, just like an alcoholic clown. In fact you'll find later, when you're putting toys away, they'll make an incredible amount of noise and sometimes even wake the baby. Thank you, technology. We had a pirate ship that would randomly let out a creepy pirate laugh whether you were playing with it or not. It started freaking us out. So we tried to take out the batteries and found out *there were no batteries in it.* The next morning we woke up and the pirate ship was gone. Occasionally you'll get a possessed toy, like that clown in *Poltergeist,* but it's rare. If you do, just take it back and get store credit.

So like I said, lots and lots of batteries. Buy batteries in bulk at Target or a discount store, but buy good ones. Cheap batteries are cheap for a reason and you'll go through the poor-quality ones fast. The last thing you want is to run out of batteries . . . for your remote.

My wife was also "nesting" at this point. She was doing extra cleaning and trying to rearrange things, and my job once the nursery was complete was to pretty much stay out of her way. But there is a male version of nesting too. And it involves big screen televisions. I recommend buying a large plasma or LCD TV and mounting it on your wall because you're not going to be leaving the house again for quite a while. Make sure it's HD and at least 50 inches. I don't care how small your room is. Some things you just can't compromise on.

Now I got pretty lucky in this regard. While my wife was pregnant, out of the blue she asked me how much "those TVs you hang on the wall" cost. I said I wasn't sure; I hadn't really priced them. Of course I had, but I wanted to see how this was going to play out. She said we should think about getting one. At that point I thought I had heard her wrong. Really? "Yes. I'm afraid our TV will fall on our baby and crush her." My first reaction was, "That's the most ridiculous thing I have ever heard." But for once I thought before speaking. Here it was. A freebie. I was *not* going to screw up a chance for an HD plasma TV. Sometimes you have to pick your battles. I calmly replied, "You're right, honey. I'm concerned for the baby's safety as well. I think that's a great idea, if only for the baby's safety. Safety is paramount—"

"Oh, shut up and check the prices online."

"Yes, ma'am!"

So I did, and we went with a Panasonic plasma television. Fifty inches of sweet, electronic, glowing, mesmerizing, high definition love. Next to having a child, it was the best thing we have ever done.

Now, to add an ironic footnote, a year after the baby was born, we read in the news that babies were being injured by falling televisions! There was actually a news report on it! I didn't believe it, but my wife was *absolutely* right. But does it really matter who is right and who is wrong? Not when you're watching *Lord of the Rings* in 1080p it doesn't. "My precious . . ."

9

The Delivery, C-sections, and Monty Python

Almost there. Almost. There were a few last-minute details to attend to and a few more unexpected decisions to make. There were a lot of loud, last-minute questions as we headed down to the nine-month wire, right when anxiety and exhaustion had my guard down. Think Michael Palin: "*Nobody* expects the Spanish Inquisition ..."

Who should be in the delivery room?

Well, you should be, for one. But after that it gets a little weird. Not in a million years did I think I would be having this conversation. Nevertheless, there I was. My wife asked me if her mother could be in the delivery room with us. I thought about it for less than one second and answered "absolutely not." The mistake I made was answering too quickly, definitively, and without explanation, and then adding, "That's the most ridiculous thing I've ever heard." Yes, mistake.

This started a whole heated discussion. "If you love me, you'll let my mother be in the delivery room."

"If you love me, you would never have asked me that."

Passive-aggressive, guilt-arguing. That's how we do it in the twenty-first century. Then I asked my wife if I could have *my* mother in the delivery room. Obviously I didn't want that either but I wanted to see her reaction. She paused, contemplated, and saw through my ruse. She didn't want that either but this was different. It was *her* mother. No one else wanted to be in the delivery room. So it was just a matter of dealing with her mother.

You have to pick your battles but I have to say this is one you should pick. The delivery room is an incredibly special time in your life. *Only the people responsible for making the child should be there.* So that's just you, your wife, and maybe your bartender. I explained to my wife that this was a very special time in our lives, and it was also a very personal one. It was one we should share together and should be a moment for just us and our new child. And about six to eight highly trained medical personnel.

Eventually she agreed. After the birth she agreed even more, and then when we described the C-section to her mother, she also agreed that it was best she hadn't been there. Keep in mind if your mother-in-law ever does agree with you, you should note the date and time.

Having the C-section like rich people

I was wondering how it would go the night of the delivery. Of course, it would be night. No one ever goes into labor during the day, right? It's always at two in the morning. Again, this is where our years of pop culture saturation work against us. I thought, would it be like the movies? It's the middle of the night, we have to race out to the hospital, I can't find the car keys, I hit my head on something, I trip over the throw rug (even though we don't have one), and then I get in the car and forget my wife. It's like a *Three Stooges* episode.

Sure, I heard stories. Then I checked with some friends who had already had children. The reality is, it is most definitely *not* like the movies. When a woman goes into labor there is a fair amount of time to get to the hospital, reducing the chance of getting stuck in traffic and having your wife deliver in the car. Or in the back of a cab by a kindhearted and knowledgeable cab driver.

Then you hear the next phase of the horror stories.

Things like, "My wife was in labor for eleven hours." Oh, my God! Can you imagine anything so horrible?! Having to *wait* for eleven hours while your wife is in labor! That's insane!

But then, for us, something funny happened on the way to the Labor. At one of the final ob-gyn visits we learned Isabella was . . . rather large and hadn't turned. The head is supposed to point toward the exit. But she wasn't in position at all. Instead, she was in the womb, sitting upright, and pretty much saying, "Come and get me, jerks." I don't know why she added "jerks" but it really felt like she did.

The doctor recommended a C-section. So wait a minute. I made him explain it in detail twice. You go in at a set time, and then the baby comes out? That's it? No labor? No late-night crazy drive in our robes? No kindhearted and knowledgeable cab driver? No labor? Score! What a time saver! So pick your birthday and enjoy.

By the way, my wife was not at all disappointed about skipping the whole labor process, especially after that horror video from the class. However, *your* wife may be disappointed about missing out on the experience of labor. If so, see if you can borrow that video.

Showtime

Sooner rather than later the big day came. And since it was scheduled, it wasn't really much of a surprise. It brought such an odd feeling. We had a scheduled appointment to have a baby. We would go to the hospital as two people and come back as three. That was crazy. We were adding a person to our household and it was happening today. It seemed so surreal.

It was a really, really weird car ride to the hospital. My wife and I both knew that this was the last spin as just a couple. The nervousness and anxiety was once again kicking in full blast, and not just for me. My wife, who wanted a baby more than anything, looked pretty nervous and pale herself. And that made *me* more nervous, which in turn made her more nervous, as I was driving. Our car became a mobile baby anxiety spiral as we drove on Highway 101.

So we got to the hospital and we had to fill out more paperwork. Wait a minute, what happened to that pre-registration?! Oh, never mind. Yes, you can make a copy of the insurance card. Hurry up!

Eventually they bring us up into one of the pre-op rooms and the pre-show begins. Seeing all the machines, I requested one that goes *ping* but there weren't any Monty Python fans on staff so they just looked at me like I was cracking under the pressure. As the nurses equally kept a close eye on me, they checked Audge's blood pressure and then with a final sonogram determined that the baby was still defiantly mocking us.

At this time the doctors and nurses did their best

to help calm us both down. Just so you know, it doesn't work. But we appreciated the effort. As they spoke to us and explained how everything was going to go down, we had to get into our costumes for the ball. Or "gowns" as they call them. I put the mask on and felt like some medical ninja from the White Gown Clan. I even took a picture in a *Karate Kid* pose to lighten the mood a little. And I think I did, for the nurses.

Nurses and doctors kept coming in and out of the room at a fast clip, but it still gave us some time alone to really let the tension mount. The anxiety was kicking and so we both tried to keep the mood light. But the truth was we were nervous and scared. We joked about if we were sure we wanted a baby. OK, I did. My wife just kind of stared at me with that look I usually get that says, "God, what is *wrong* with you?"

Our next visitor was the anesthesiologist, although I was disappointed to find out it was for my wife and not me, but whatever. Our doctor then came in to reassure us and let us know there is nothing to worry about and that this is all routine. Sure, for him. For us it was kind of a big deal.

There was a lot more prep time before the actual event, which meant we both continued to sit in a room together while the hospital staff giggled in the other room and made bets if either of us was going to pass out. That, and I think they prepare the operating room.

Then after what seemed like days they came in and got my wife. We both knew that in a few moments everything was about to change. You just feel it in your soul. I had been feeling the usual fear and anxiety up to this point. But now time slowed down and I felt the familiar fear and anxiety mixed with anticipation, adrenaline, and maybe even a little gas.

In the delivery room

A little bit of time went by and then a nurse came in to bring me into the delivery room. My wife was all set up on the table and I went to go stand by her head. They had a nice large curtain strategically placed so it blocked both our views as to what they were doing to get the baby out. Let me just say, thank you. I wonder what happened the day before they started that practice? I'm sure it involved throwing up, passing out, and things needing to be sterilized over and over.

I stayed by my wife's head the whole time because the last thing I wanted to witness was strangers cutting into her and yanking out a child. There are some things you are just not meant to see. It's like pushing the button on the puzzle box from *Hellraiser*. No, thank you. I have enough nightmares. I don't need any more.

And so it began. Audge was holding my hand rather

tightly, to the point where I had to get some help from the nurse as I was losing circulation in my fingers. What's amazing is how quiet the surgery is. They had the radio on, which was weird but kinda cool because they had it set to the alternative station. My baby was being born to Alice in Chains. You really don't hear any of the cutting or anything. Again, thank you.

By natural childbirth or a C-section, that baby is finally here. Our new child's crying was the first loud sound we heard in that operating room. The baby is pulled out, hits the air, begins to scream, and the sound immediately touches your very soul. It's one of the most defining moments of your life and it involves a lot of screaming. Actually, most of the defining moments of our lives involve screaming. Whether it's out loud or in our heads, quietly building up, all of our life-defining moments are represented by that Edvard Munch painting. At that point I wondered if I had saved any sedatives or Zoloft tablets from my drug-happy psychiatrist. That was silly. Of course I had.

The nurses wrapped the baby and brought her past the horror curtain and over to Mommy's head for the first time. Through her drug-induced haze she looked at this little baby covered in viscous goo and instantly fell in love with her. I have to say it was the happiest I have ever seen my wife. Even happier than on her wedding day when there were just so many tears (of joy, I'm sure), especially on her side of the family.

Now, some people will tell you that when you see your baby for the first time, you will instantly love him or her. I'm sure for some people that's true. It was certainly true for my wife. Not so much for me. It was most certainly not love at first sight. I was in too much shock to feel much of anything. I just looked at this screaming little monkey covered in *Ghostbusters* slime and if anything, I felt a detachment. Like my brain was saying, "OK, we're at the outskirts of crazytown about now. I'm going to shut down for a bit while you get all this sorted."

The whole delivery room experience was so surreal I felt like I'd walked into a Monty Python sketch. From the machine that goes *ping* that they *finally* brought in to thinking about ex-parrots, SPAM, and silly walks. But after one last thought of "I am your king." "Well, I didn't vote for you . . ." it was back to reality. Soon I was once again looking at my new daughter as the nurse held her.

Then they brought Isabella over to the cleaning table where they weighed her and asked me if I wanted to cut the cord.

"Is it covered by insurance?" I asked.

"Er, yes."

"Then you do it."

The nurses then looked at me and asked *me* if I was

OK. I must have gone as pale as Katie Holmes at her first Scientology mixer as I looked at this little oily, wrinkled, screaming Cabbage Patch doll that a few seconds ago had been inside my wife. How would anyone react? I don't get any credit for not running away screaming. Again, Munch's painting came to mind. Sure, the final version was on a bridge, but the original one was probably in a delivery room.

I really just wanted to pass out at this point but they kind of frown upon that in the maternity ward. So they took my daughter away to the nursery and I was about to follow when I thought of something I had forgotten in the chaos. I asked the doctor if he could do the "father stitch" on my wife. If you don't know what that is, let me explain: When a woman has a baby, a certain part of her anatomy let's say gets larger during the birth to accommodate the child being born. Sometimes that part . . . tears and needs to be sewn back up. The "father stitch" is that one extra stitch for the father. I asked the doctor if he would do it.

"But, sir, your wife had a C-section."

"So?"

10

The Hospital Stay and Unexpected Epiphanies

I followed my child into the nursery as the doctors sewed my wife back up. Audge was pretty out of it from the drugs so she probably thought I was still in there with her anyway. I looked at my child flailing around in her new plastic holder. It looked like she had just come out of a vending machine. Is it just me or do they keep the babies in trays that look disturbingly similar to those bins you put your belongings on in an airport security line? No time to think about that now.

I watched the nurses do all these tests, measurements, shots, and stuff to my child. Since we're in LA, they even took her headshot photo, which was nice. The shock was starting to wear off and the haze beginning to clear. Isabella was born with a full head of hair! I thought babies were supposed to be born bald?! OK, we are both Italian so it wasn't that much of a shock. My first task as a new father was to wash my child's hair. With the nurses' help, of course. Don't worry, the nurses are all smart enough to know not to leave you alone with the baby. We went over to the sink and washed my daughter's hair. It was unexpected and kind of nice. Our first bonding experience.

Soon the nurses took over and I went back into the hospital room and waited for the doctor to bring my wife back. If it's a C-section, it's going to take a little more time. At this point came an added distraction that we didn't need or want. Kind of like when NBC remade *Knight Rider*. Audge's father kept calling right after the delivery and the nurse kept coming in and asking, "Are you taking any calls yet?" and I had to keep telling the nurse we would call back as soon as we could. The baby was just delivered and Audge was slowly being moved to the hospital bed and her gown had a lot of blood on it. The last thing I wanted to do was leave the room to talk to her father.

If you live far away from your family, they may try to start calling the hospital. Tell them *not* to. Tell them you'll call them. The hospital can't give out any information due to privacy laws so they will try and get the info from you as soon as they can. This means calling every thirty seconds like a teenager trying to score weed.

Tell your family to lay off the phone for a bit. *You'll call them* when everything settles down. And you should only need to call one family member. They should then spread the word to both families for you. That's right; use the baby phone chain.

Welcome to the maternity ward. Make yourself comfortable. Stay a while.

I knew I was going to be spending the next few days in my wife's hospital room, so I tried to settle in. In case you were wondering, the hospital clichés all still apply. The food is god-awful, make sure you have good insurance, and don't fall asleep or they'll chemically induce a coma and sell your organs. But mainly the food is awful. So try to bring your wife some healthy goodies. Her diet will be restricted for a bit or she may not have much of an appetite. *May* is the key word here. If you want to start an argument, you could always start your conversation with, "But I thought you weren't supposed to—" All women are different and she may want nothing but chocolate. You better get it; but try to sneak some fruit or protein in there too.

The amount of time spent in the hospital will vary due to the nature of the birth. A C-section will always keep you in a little longer, about four days after the surgery. And my wife really needed that extra time. She was not in great shape at this point. You should do your best to make her as comfortable as possible. In exchange it will be more comfortable for you when you finally get home. Think of it as a comfort exchange.

Most hospitals now have private rooms for new mothers with a cot or something for the husband to stay over. Our hospital, however, did not and we even had to share a room. Supposedly there was a new maternity wing being built, but it wasn't ready yet. Due to the uncomfortable overcrowding I was not allowed to stay over. I had to go home every night! It was awful. I had to keep going home every night to our empty and quiet house where no one would bother me. Yes, I kept telling my wife how awful it was.

Now, there is also an added educational bonus at the hospital. Turns out the nurses know a lot more about taking care of an infant than you do. Think of them as a walking *Encyclopedia Infantica*. Use them as a resource. Hell, you're paying for it. Get your money's worth. They will teach you how to put the diapers on properly and how to swaddle the child. It's much different from the classes. Mainly because the child is actually moving around now and being a bit loud about things. It's disconcerting at first. Our baby was not cooperating at all the way the immobile piece of plastic had.

The nurses know all and can help you with everything from feeding to answering questions like, "Is she *supposed* to do that?" You learn more about care of your infant in a few days from the nurses than you will from hours and hours of those long, boring classes. And thankfully they won't show you one horror-inducing movie. But this doesn't get you out of that infant CPR class. You really should still take that one. Quit trying to get out of it.

The hospital stay will actually go pretty quickly for you and your wife. We found each day was a blur of nurses, pills, baby care, learning about changing diapers (again), getting phone calls and flower bouquets from family, and, of course, sleeping. Then we'd do it all over again the next day.

It was the second or third day in the hospital when it hit me. I was sitting there quietly in an uncomfortable hospital chair and holding my new daughter. I looked at her. *That* was the moment. The moment I fell in love with my child. It wasn't in the delivery room and it wasn't instantly. It took a couple of days but when it happened, it happened. I don't even think my wife noticed. She was too hopped up on painkillers to catch anything except that I had stolen her brownie from her hospital dinner.

From that moment on I knew in my heart that I was now a father and this was *my* child. Mine. *And the thought no longer terrified me.* Here she was. I looked at her again and thought: "This little human being, cuddled in my arms, was what I was so afraid of? Why?" Suddenly all of my reasons for being freaked out about having a child didn't seem as important anymore. She was starting to fall asleep and looked so incredibly peaceful.

A genetic switch had gone off inside me. As I held my child, I realized that caring for her would be difficult, but not impossible. And I could do it. Of course I could. In fact, I was going to do it well. She deserved nothing less.

This whole transformation that's going to come over you is very personal, and you're going to have to experience it for yourself. There are no words to really describe it. But when you have this combination of epiphany and metamorphosis, you'll know it. Like if Franz Kafka had just eaten a bowl of chocolate ice cream. No matter how bleak and oppressive things seem, when you're eating a delicious bowl of refreshing chocolate ice cream, even Kafka would have to admit that things aren't so bad.

I had just become a father, and gotten through it OK. And it really wasn't so bad. It's as if I had accomplished one of the things I've been put on this earth to do. Genetically speaking, I had, I suppose. Imagine doing one thing in your life you're actually supposed to do. Weird. Meaning of life stuff. Although, like I said earlier, it felt more like *Monty Python's The Meaning of Life* stuff at the time, but meaning of life nevertheless. Who knew comic surrealism and biological reproduction were so intricately entwined?

I looked at my daughter again as she slept in my arms. She was truly adorable. Everyone thinks that their own baby is beautiful. But I'm telling you my daughter was much prettier than all of the other ugly, ugly babies in the nursery. But hey, they were someone else's problem.

So . . . Now What Do We Do?

I've spent a fair amount of the book leading up to and talking about the birth, mainly because this seems to be where the bulk of our mind-numbing pre-baby anxiety lies. Before the baby is here, most of our adjustments are all mental. Not really our strong suit. When the baby finally got here, I was so exhausted from being a basket case that it was actually a relief. Once the baby was in front of me I finally had something tangible to worry about. That was much easier.

Our exciting new life together was about to begin. Of course, there was one little hurdle before we started that whole new life together: We actually had to get that baby home. It hit me as we were exiting the hospital and about to get into the car, the three of us, for the first time: I looked at the baby car seat and realized I had no idea how to put the baby in this Byzantine restraining device.

All I can tell you is that you should practice before you even get to the hospital. Buy a freaking doll and strap it in. I'm not kidding. The car-seat straps look like diabolical tethers designed by Erno Rubik. There are like *fifty* of them and they all have to be adjusted to your child's height and weight, which of course is impossible until the baby is actually in it. So you have to make your best guess.

I had everything hooked up and then put the baby in the car seat. Or at least I tried. After we got home I checked the manual for the one hundredth time and it turns out I had the straps connected completely wrong. So we made our first mistake with the baby before she was even home. Yes, I know, well done. At least the baby was now home and in front of me so I could adjust the straps properly. By the way, do that *immediately*. Like even before you drink a bottle of vodka and pass out. Which you will do, when it sinks in that the baby is finally here and in your house.

Okay, we got the baby home. Check. We put the baby in the living room in the Pack 'n Play. This was a defining moment in our lives, and we both knew it. My wife and I looked at our new baby, then looked at each other, and we were both silent for a bit. Finally I looked at my wife and said, "Now what do we do?"

That's the feeling you have when you get your baby home for the first time. I remember us just kind of sitting there, looking at the baby as if she were going to tell us what to do. Like she was going to say, "Stop staring at me and get moving. Feed me, change me, sterilize the pacifiers, and put my blankets in a neat pile over there. Let's go, chop chop."

Those first few weeks, as you get your baby sea legs, everything feels ethereal and dreamlike, mainly because of lack of sleep. You may even start to hallucinate. One night I really felt like I was in a production of *The Pirates of Penzance* with pacifiers. "Honey, Major-General Stanley wants his bottle *now*." At all times of the day or night, without an intermission, your child will eat, sleep, and poop. That's about it for a while. 24/7. Of course I wondered how doing just three things can take up so much time, but it does. It's the mystery of the baby time-space continuum.

During the first few weeks we had the baby in a bassinet usually right next to Audge's side of the bed. This made waking up and breastfeeding easier, especially since my wife had had a C-section. She was still recovering and wasn't able to lift the baby or move too much. Or she was faking it. Either way, I went with it.

Here is something that caught us completely off guard. Babies make crazy noises in their sleep. And they don't even wake up when they're doing it. We'd be sleeping and this awful wail would come from the bassinet and when we looked over, Isabella was sound asleep. Then we thought we were hearing things or maybe being *Punk'd* by an infant ventriloquist.

Babies will indeed make inhuman shrieks and groans without ever waking up. Either your child just made a crazy wail or your neighbor just clubbed a baby seal. That's what it sounds like. I suppose it's the baby's way of saying, "From now on it's all about me. Even when I'm asleep. Just wanted to remind you. I'll be quiet now for roughly the next nine minutes. Use them wisely."

This is where family can be a huge help. If they are around to offer support, by all means, exploit them. Since all of our immediate family was back east, a few days after the birth Audge's mom came to help out and then my mother came out after that for a week. It was a *huge* help. Your family will want to see the new baby and you can easily trick them into doing some of the care. It's like you're Tom Sawyer and your baby is a fence that needs painting.

When a visiting relative wants to or is tricked into doing the feedings for a few nights, God bless them. After the baby is born and you actually get a good, full night's sleep, you'll feel like you've won the freaking lottery.

You're just going to need a little help right now. From

taking care of the baby to food shopping, you and your wife are going to be too busy or too tired to do everything. Something as simple as answering the phone becomes a big deal during this time. People are calling all the time to see how the baby is doing and yet you have no time to talk or even answer the phone. Let one of your friends or family members handle that. You'll find that will help a lot. It did until my friend pretended to be me and told a telemarketer he was going to come down there and kick his stupid annoying ass. That wasn't as helpful. Then again, the telemarketer never called back.

Eventually the event I had not been looking forward to happened. Our relatives all went home and my wife wanted to leave the house by herself for a few hours. That's right. There's no getting around it. Sooner or later you're going to be home alone with the baby. Don't panic. Plus, if you screw up, it's not like the baby is going to tell on you. Just make sure your wife hasn't turned on the nanny cam before she leaves.

So there I was, alone with my baby for the first time. I looked at my daughter and she looked back at me with a slightly worried look on her face. Like she was saying, "I like you and all, but where's the other one?" I was nervous but I got through it OK. Feeding, changing, holding. Got it. As long as the diaper holds, we're in business. It's when they have that accident when you're alone that we panic.

It's like your infant just exploded a "dirty bomb." That first time, you just think to yourself, "OK, I could clean the poop off the baby, clean the poop off me, clean the poop off the floor, clean the poop off the walls, or I could just hang myself."

Sometimes this is just a test and you'll find your wife never left the driveway. She just wanted to make sure nothing caught fire and the house was still there after ten minutes and there were no news vans pulling up. Good for her.

These first few months are a special and unusual time in your lives, and we realized it. Even more so than when we got the 50-inch plasma television. We tried to take as much time off work as possible. If you or your wife can afford to take a family leave for a few months, take it. Especially your wife, who will probably want to stay home as long as possible. We did five months. Federal law has a Family and Medical Leave Act and many states have their own similar laws that allow about twelve weeks of leave. All or a portion of it is paid, depending on where you live and what your employer allows. As much as I'd like to help you out here, I'm not a lawyer. You're going to have to check on that yourself.

Her employer must hold her job for her during any legally mandated leave. She'll have to check with her job, and they will send her to Human Resources hell as punishment for asking for so much time off. Audge went through so many departments inside her company that it felt like the maternity leave was outsourced by the outsourced department and then hidden in an underground HR lair accessible only by hunched over gnomes with BlackBerry smartphones.

Even though we were completely sleep deprived and semiconscious most of the time, we both knew and felt the specialness of this time together. I even looked forward to the late-night, exhaustion-induced musical hallucinations, especially when the Pirate King would come to visit and sing his "Pirate King Song." We knew this time wouldn't last very long and that we would never have this time again with Mother, Father, and baby. We would go back to work and Isabella would get older. So to belabor a point here, while your house has just been turned upside down, try to slow down and enjoy this special time together with the three of you. Don't worry, something annoying will happen either at work or somewhere else soon enough to get you crazy, but for now enjoy spending as much time as you can inside your new family bubble.

Also, this is a special bonding time for mommy and baby, especially if there is breastfeeding involved. Audge seemed to need this bonding time just as much as the baby. It's very, very important. She loved just being with the new baby and would still have that glow when they were together. I almost played Neil Diamond's "Heartlight" during one of these times, but that song is difficult to enjoy even on an ironic level.

Mommy should be the one who is the primary caregiver at the very beginning of your child's life. I'm not saying that just because I hate changing diapers, which I do; I'm just saying that's what the experts said. In other words, whenever you want to get out of work, quote experts. And never, *ever* let your wife uncover the fact that there is a large, male-expert conspiracy to help us get out of doing stuff. If they do, then it's all over.

My Baby Is Crying.
Help Me.

Babies cry for various reasons. But I soon learned that they're really not as complicated as we're led to believe. It's like learning to make your own website. It sounds hard at first but then you realize that porn stars do it all the time. It just takes a little practice.

If your baby is crying, all you have to do is run down a small checklist to figure it out. What's crazy is that while there aren't that many things, because you haven't slept in what feels like twenty years you forget things on the list, the order, or even whose baby it is that you're holding. So make a chart and put it on the fridge next to the phone numbers of Poison Control, your pediatrician's emergency number, and takeout places that deliver after 2:00 a.m.

1. Hungry

Feed your baby. Seems like a no-brainer, but like I said, some nights you won't have full usage of said brain, so refer to said chart.

2. Gas

There may be a burp in there. Did you try to get it out? Sitting up, over the shoulder, try all the burping positions. Baby gas can cause lots of discomfort. Throughout the house. If the gas is chronic, you can also try something called gripe water for infants. Sometimes it works. Sometimes. Of course, if it doesn't, this may lead you to the adult gripe water for yourself, or "whiskey," as it's commonly referred to.

3. Change

Sometimes babies don't want to sit in their own filth. Sometimes they do. This predicament would not bother our daughter Isabella at all. She would happily sit in a dirty diaper as long as she was fed. It bothered me, though. It bothered me that it didn't bother her. But then again, I'm easily bothered. So we probably changed her a little too often. "This diaper is dry but it's too foldy. I'll change it."

4. May just want a pacifier

Babies like to suck. It's the only thing they do, really. They do it for practical reasons and for recreation. So they may just want a little recreational sucking and may not be hungry. So if he just wants the pacifier, don't try and shove the bottle in his mouth. He'll get angry. Oh, so very angry.

5. Too hot or too cold

Not quite as obvious, but feel the hands and feet for cold and look for a red flushiness in the face if too hot. I remember Isabella waking up in the middle of the night and us not figuring it out until we wrapped her up in another blanket and held her. She gave us a look, and we deserved it.

6. Wants to sleep and can't settle

Babies can need help going to sleep. It seems so easy, right? We can do it all the time, anywhere, even at work. Babies don't have those skills yet. Try rocking or using the pacifier to help your baby learn how to sleep. That's right, teach him how it's done. Just remember to put him on his back. There's a "back to sleep" movement endorsed by the American Academy of Pediatrics and other organizations to reduce SIDS (Sudden Infant Death Syndrome). Also, no pillows or thick blankets. Same reason. Wow, I actually snuck a little actual information in there. That may happen periodically.

7. Wants to be held

Sometimes a baby just wants to be held. But don't we all?

8. Illness

Your baby may be sick. He's no happier about it than you are. You have your pediatrician's phone number in a convenient place, right? Right?

9. Wants you to leave her alone

Babies can get overstimulated and need some time to settle and sleep. So sometimes those big scary adults making all of those weird noises need to back off a little bit. Seriously. I'm not making this one up.

10. Teething

Generally, teething doesn't really start until around six months *but* you just may have an overachiever on your hands. Drooling? Cranky? Irritable? Biting everything? Now check your baby. If your baby has any of these symptoms, it may be teething. We used teething tablets and they worked great. You can also give your baby a teether to chew on, or even your finger, if you're a masochist.

None of the above?

Wow. Now what? Try the old standby: motion. You can try anything from carrying the baby around to putting the baby in a swing. Er, a *baby* swing. Of course, there is always the last resort: a lovely, scenic drive at four in the morning.

Now, if none of these things work it may be colic, which there is not a lot you can do about. However, there are some things you can do to try and reduce the severity—like gripe water—and if you're breastfeeding, change your wife's diet. Now, she is obviously not going to believe you if you tell her this, so you're going to have to wait while she checks with her friends and the doctor for verification. My wife was drinking coffee, and caffeine can cause stomach distress in the baby via breast milk. She eliminated coffee from her diet, albeit reluctantly, and within a day our child had less gas pains. Magic.

Now, if your baby is still crying and it's not any of these things and it's not colic, then you have obviously done something to piss off your baby. Apologize and try again.

Now That I Have Another Mouth to Feed, How Do I Feed It?

First lesson I learned: Damn, babies are hungry. And they get really angry if you don't feed them right away. It's like they're saying, "Look, I only need one thing, and you know I need it. What could possibly be taking so long?" This leads us to the big question:

Boob or Bottle?

Let me just say the longer your child can be on breast milk, the better. For you. It's less work and your wife is freaking making it. You don't even have to go out and get it. But I hear it's also good for the baby, apparently. He is getting lots of nutrients and antibodies from the mother's milk. For the first few days the baby gets something called *colostrum*. This is "supermilk" that has a huge amount of nutrients, antibodies, and a fresh minty taste. That's why it's important to start breastfeeding right away. At least that's what *everyone* kept telling us.

Here's where we got all of the advice shoved down our throats again. Other parents, our doctors, and the Internet told us how great it is to breastfeed and how you're a negligent parent if you don't. Breastfed babies are smarter, although I have no idea how you would measure that unless maybe you had twins and only gave one of them breast milk. I don't remember hearing about any studies of that nature or seeing a postnatal woman with one giant engorged breast but maybe I'm not looking hard enough.

Audge wanted as much info about breastfeeding as she could find. I remember one time when she was pregnant and discussing breastfeeding with a few of the new moms at a party. I walked in on the middle of the conversation and all I heard was "cracked, bloody nipples." As you can imagine, I didn't need to hear any more. I immediately turned away and left the room with my hands over my ears, reciting "John Jacob Jingleheimer Schmidt."

But here's the best part about breastfeeding: It doesn't matter. It's really not *your* decision. You're not the one with the breasts. And if you are, then go to the gym. Anyway, your wife will pretty much decide whether she's going to breastfeed or not. And she's not going to hear another word about it. So there you go. Got out of another one. Or so it would seem.

The first few feedings, my wife looked like she was in heaven bonding with our child. By breastfeeding, she bonded with Isabella the way only a mother and baby can—by squirting milk out of an engorged mammary gland into a ravenous infant's mouth. This is something we men will never understand and you know what? That's fine. Not something we really *want* to understand.

But like that new car smell, eventually your wife's love of being there for every feeding will wear off. So what now? Once again, our fair-weather friend science comes back to punch us men in the face. Enter the breast pump, another invention to give more work to men. Now your baby can have breast milk without the breast! It's easy, fast, and fun! Actually, it's none of those things. Breast pumps are ugly torture devices that are slow, loud, and sometimes painful. To watch. I'm not really sure how it is for the woman. Still, eventually your wife will want to play Borg Queen and meld with the machine. That milk is coming out and it's waiting for you. Ask not for whom the Breast Pump tolls. It tolls for thee.

Sometimes there's extra milk from the pump. What

do you do with it? You can't just throw it away. We played Truth or Dare with it. It puts a whole new nutritious spin on the game.

My wife wanted to pump so I could help out with the late-night feedings. OK, fine; that's only fair. So I did my duty and you know what? It was kind of nice. The house was completely quiet, I had a little bonding time with my daughter as I fed her, changed her, and then slowly rocked her back to sleep. You may be tempted to turn the TV on but I have to say try not to. Nowadays we never really get to enjoy the quiet anymore. You could even put one of those lullaby CDs on if it will help your baby get back to sleep, but I recommend taking this time to just relax, bond, and not listen to any electronic noise.

Now I'm not saying this is how I felt at every feeding. There were some nights I was so tired I just did not want to get out of that nice warm bed. There are a few other things you can try. I found I could get out of a few feedings if I faked being in a deep sleep. My wife would then get up and do the feedings because she's up at that point anyway and had given up trying to wake me. Unfortunately, this ruse only works for so long and sooner or later she will catch on. The nudging will get harder and more painful and eventually you'll have to get up and do your share.

Another ploy to try is saying "your turn" when your

wife is half asleep and the baby is crying. She'll be so groggy from lack of sleep that she'll already be in the baby's room before she realizes she's been duped. Like I said, you may only get to use these tactics once or twice, so make the most of your few extra stolen moments of precious sleep.

But that's all I have, so at this point you're on your own. Maybe you'll think of some other ways to get out of late-night feedings. Be creative. I mean, when you get right down to it, marriage and parenting really just boil down to threat assessment and avoidance, manipulation, and delegation through manipulation.

Life after breastfeeding

Soon your baby will be ready for baby food. Judging by the copious diversity of baby food available, I thought our baby would be on baby food for years. Nope. In total, giving your child baby food lasts only for a couple of months. I know, I couldn't believe it either. Baby food is really just a stopgap transition from milk to table food. It starts at around six months and ends at around a year, give or take a month or two.

And yet for those few months there were rows and rows of tiny little jars, just sitting on the shelf and mocking me. They were daring me to pick the right ones. So what's good and what isn't? Once again, pop culture to the rescue. I learned all I need to know about baby food by listening to the cartoon characters.

A good rule of thumb is that if a PBS character is on the box, like Elmo or Clifford, that generally means healthier food. But you have to watch those wily cartoon characters. While recently companies have made more of an attempt to make kid food with happy, smiling cartoon characters healthier, you need to check the ingredients of everything you give your child. Avoid the sugar and chemical rush at meal times and you won't have to wait for your child to "come down" before you put him to bed.

Even for that brief 4–6 months of baby food, it gets split up again into subroutines of baby food stages. At around six months you can start the process. First, you'll start off with rice cereal mixed with breast milk or formula. It will get them ready for food and it may even help them sleep longer at night because their bellies will be fuller. Win-win. But check with your pediatrician and see what they say.

Actually, you should check with your pediatrician about everything. It's not a bad habit to get into. Well, not everything; I mean, don't be a nag. But stuff like, "What should I feed my kid?" and, "What's that thing on his butt?" are all legitimate questions.

So what is the difference between baby food stages,

other than a seemingly arbitrary numbering system of 1–3? Here is all you need to know to become a baby foodie:

Stage 1

This is the pureed stuff that's pretty much what babies and overly enthusiastic bodybuilders eat. Seriously. Sometimes I get really bored and investigate rumors I've heard on the Internet. There are indeed resources for bodybuilders who eat baby food. Go ahead, ask the Internet. Anyway, back to the baby. Try to get organic, if you can, to avoid additives and chemicals. If you want to save money, you could just make your own baby food too. All you really need is a good food processor. The only difference is the jar. But really, who has time for that?

As you're introducing new foods at this point, watch for allergic reactions. Trust me; you'll know. Swelling, rash, etc. Same things you used to look for two days after spring break. Also, try to give lots of vegetables and limit the sweet fruits. You don't want to give your baby a taste for sweets right away. It's a hard habit to break. Believe me. In fact, as I'm writing this, I just ate a Tastykake Peanut Butter Kandy Kake. The most awesome snack cake ever. It's a Philly thing.

Stage 2

This is mushy but has some texture. It's for the baby who's just learning to chew and may have a few teeth. Nothing else to report here. Stage two is the most uneventful of the baby food stages.

Stage 3

Depending on the effort put forth by the baby food maker, this stage is either chunky baby food or just actual food shoved into a baby food jar. More of a marketing gimmick than anything else.

Regardless of the stage, your baby is not going to eat neatly. And you know what? That's fine. They're still exploring their environments and don't understand that food doesn't go on the ceiling until college. At this stage the only way to keep your kitchen clean is if you buy a lot of plastic and prepare it *Dexter* style.

The one really positive thing we noticed about trying to have our child eat healthily is that my wife and I were starting to eat healthier. We tried to get as many food additives, chemicals, and processed foods out of our house. And you know what? We actually started to feel better too as all of those toxins and chemicals left our systems.

The problem is, eating healthier costs a lot more. We had to take out a second mortgage just so we could shop at Whole Foods Market. When as a society did we get to the point where it costs more to get less shit in our food? Like the supermarkets are saying, "You want food that's not going to kill you? Now that's gonna cost ya . . ."

And once you have the better tasting, less chemically processed food, it's hard to go back. All-natural peanut butter actually tastes like peanuts. But it's a downward spiral. Soon you start jonesing for that organic pear and that grain-fed, free-range chicken. Next thing you know it's four in the morning and you're banging on the door at Trader Joe's. "Come on, man, just a few grapes. I'll pay you next week, I swear . . ."

The Myths and Truths of Having a Child

When you're having a child, all of a sudden everyone around you suddenly becomes a wise old guru living on top of a mountain eager to dispense timeless advice on parenting and child care. From the telephone guy to your friends at work, they just repeat canned phrases they've heard but never really noticed have very little basis in reality. It's not even advice. It's more like parental sound-bite clichés.

Mainly it comes from people who don't have children and who you barely know. I'm not sure why that happens, but it does. The less you know the person, the dumber the saying. I have collected a list of the most egregiously annoying parental sayings and will tell you if they are true or not.

There's no best time to have a child.

This first piece of advice has little bearing on reality. Just look at the opposite for a moment. What are some of the worst times to have a child? When you're too young or too old? You can't provide for her financially? You're going to be on the next season of *Survivor*? If you want truth, the saying should be changed to "There are plenty of horrible times to have a child."

Pregnant women are beautiful.

Yes, especially when they're screaming at you for something you did four years ago. Everyone knows pregnant women are *not* beautiful. They are large, moody, loud, and hungry. Think final scene from *Aliens*. And I'm not talking about Sigourney Weaver. Saying pregnant women are beautiful is just a clever and useful tactic to calm pregnant women down. The first man who used that phrase was a very wise fellow who just wanted to get some sleep. That's it.

No man finds a pregnant woman beautiful. That's the truth. And if he does, he has serious psychological problems best left to professionals to sort out. And I think this is perfectly fine and the way nature intended it. I think it's nature's way of saying to the male, "Someone beat you to it. Stay away from this one." And we do. Gladly. It's nature's perfect harmony. Why fight it?

The first year goes by so fast.

Bullshit. You're sleeping six hours *less* a night, you have no idea what you're doing, and your wife doesn't want to have sex anymore. How does this make things go *quicker*?! That first year, it feels like a year. And then some.

When it's your own baby, you'll feel differently about kids.

I have to say this one is half true. I still find other people's kids annoying and I don't really want to be around them. In fact, I still find a lot of other people annoying and I don't want to be around them. But when it is your own kid, all the rules change.

I think it's genetically programmed into us. When Isabella was born, I wanted to do everything I could to care for her and make her feel comfortable. It really bothered me when she was crying. When my own child cries, I feel horrible and want to do whatever I can to help her feel better. When I hear a neighbor's child cry, I just think *somebody* please *shut that kid up*.

The opposite is also true. When your child does something, it's cute. When another child does the exact same thing, it is mildly amusing but then borders on annoying. Still, when your wife's friends are over with their kids, you are really going to have to feign interest. Do it correctly this time. You remember what happened during the "getting the baby's room ready" phase, don't you? Let's not have a repeat.

Sooner or later your car is going to smell like throw up.

OK, this is one I'm adding, and it's absolutely true. It's going to happen. Maybe not today, maybe not tomorrow, but soon. I dodged the bullet for a while and our daughter only threw up in my wife's car. I was sure it was her driving. She, however, disagreed rather loudly. I don't know why I even suggested it. You know that voice in your head that says, "You really shouldn't say that" right before you say something? Mine is broken.

Soon the throw-up karma caught up with me. When Isabella was about twenty months old, we were *two* blocks from daycare and *thar she blows*.

The entire morning milk feeding came back up as curdled cottage cheese. Now here is the main difference between you and your wife. When your child projectile vomits in the car, your wife's first reaction will always be,

"My baby!" *Your* first reaction will always be, "My car!" So now your car smells like throw up, just like when you were in college.

Now, as a bonus, I'm going to give you some *very* helpful advice when this happens. This will save you the embarrassment of calling your wife, like I did, and saying, "What do I do?"

Leave the . . . *slippery* . . . child in the car seat once you're home for one second. Run in and get a towel. Or better yet, leave a large towel in your car. There. If you read this chapter in time, you just saved a step. Wrap the child in the towel and then bring him inside and then right into the bathtub or changing table. This will prevent the baby's semiliquid gift from getting on your clothes or the floor. You'll save about two hours in cleanup time. You're welcome.

I'll never see my friends again.

This is a popular verbal dirge of the soon-to-be father. Didn't you say that when you got married? Then a few months later your wife said, "Why are your friends always over here?"

This is going to be up to you. We had friends over on Sundays to watch HBO shows like *The Sopranos, Carnivàle,* and *Deadwood* and now we have them over to watch *Dexter* on Showtime. Take that, HBO. If you make the effort, you can still see your friends. It's just more effort. Plus, some of them may already have kids or be having kids of their own soon so it will be even more effort, but possible.

Remember, your single friends may not really know how to react to your having a child. They may not call because they think you want to stay in with your family for the rest of your life now. Assure them that's not the case. You do still like to go out to dinner or to the movies on occasion. Maybe even a bar. But you'll be so tired that after one beer you'll think someone slipped you a mickey.

So make seeing your friends an event. Schedule that poker night. Way in advance, of course. Now it has to be on the calendar. Whoever gets the event on the calendar first wins. Remember you'll be competing with baby showers, hair appointments, chick flicks, and an occasional bachelorette party. Verbal commitments don't count. It has to be in writing. And I would write it in with a Sharpie. If you use a pencil, you're just asking to be bumped for the next *Sex and the City* movie.

Getting together with your buddies will take on a whole new meaning. "Guys night out" is what you'll call it, which is ironic because all you'll really be doing is staying in and talking about how you used to go out.

It's hard to imagine your life without kids.

Really? Try it. It's actually very easy. You're sleeping late, you're going out to dinner with your wife, you're going to the movies at the drop of a hat, and you're planning a trip to New Zealand to finally take that *Lord of the Rings* tour that you've wanted to take since the first movie came out. That wasn't so hard.

But then, as you're imagining these things, you actually feel that something is missing. There is an odd emptiness in your pre-child life. It's weird, and it's definitely one of those things you never really understand until you have a child.

I remember feeling nostalgic about that time in my life where I could just do whatever I wanted when I wanted, but as time progressed, I began missing that time less and less. As I watched Isabella grow, I knew it was really such a small sacrifice. That pre-child time became a stage in my life, like any other, and it was time that it was over. And I stretched it out longer than most people, believe me.

I really think life is a series of stages, in every sense of the word. Whether you're performing on one or moving on to the next one. At each new stage in our lives, there are new things to look forward to but you always have to leave something behind. If I may get all philosophical for a moment, what we gain is sometimes defined by what we are giving up. Growth and change are scary and often difficult, but ultimately good for us.

I mean, what if Frodo had stayed in the Shire all his life? He wouldn't have saved the world, but more important, he would have been bored and regretful, wondering what his life may have been like if he had just helped that weird old man in the hat take a ring somewhere. So don't be afraid of change and new stages. Embrace your inner hobbit.

15

Picking a Daycare, or When to Give Your Child to a Complete Stranger

At the end of Audrey's maternity leave we were faced with a decision. It's the same decision every new parent makes when the maternity leave runs out. Unless you or your wife is going to stay home and care for your child, you're going to have to get some outside help. And calling *Nanny 911* doesn't count. Apparently. Audge and I live in California, and both of our families are in either Pennsylvania or New Jersey. Mainly because they love paying tolls. So needless to say, family wasn't really an option for us.

Lucky for us, nowadays there are many exciting ways you can pass off the care of your child to someone you barely know. But we had absolutely no idea how to go about picking one. I kept hearing the same advice from books, family, and friends over and over: *"You have to do what's best for you and your family."* Wow, what a safe, nonthreatening, and ultimately useless bon mot of advice. That helps me in no way whatsoever. That was my initial reaction anyway. After examining the options and going through the process, I hate to admit it was ultimately good advice.

Every family is different and requires a solution specific to them. Everything is a factor, including cost. Families use nannies, have grandparents or other family members who are willing to be abused, or use daycare. Some even build time-traveling robots that slide back and forth in time to anticipate a baby's needs so they never cry. How cool would that be? Anyway, since we couldn't get time-traveling robots—yet—we used daycare. Also because my wife and I love being sick. But more on that later.

We got lucky choosing a daycare. Or I should say we *thought* we got lucky. You know what they say about the best-laid plans . . . We heard great things about a daycare facility close to where Audrey works. We scheduled a tour, and Audrey's mother was visiting at the time so we brought her too. Our first visit ever to a daycare facility and with my mother-in-law tagging along. What could possibly go wrong?

We didn't really know what to expect. But when we got to this daycare and took a look around, we couldn't believe our eyes. It was rows and rows of classrooms with cement walls. It had to be acres. It wasn't a daycare; it was a farm. I was appalled. Aldous Huxley wouldn't send his kid here. But like I said, we had never visited a daycare before, so what the hell? We didn't know. Maybe they're all like this. So we went in for the tour.

We began touring the growth cells, er, rooms, and it became more and more dystopian. I could swear our tour guide said, "When the individual feels, the community reels." Then again, maybe she just said, "This way, please." She was one of those authoritative women who thought we wanted to hear about every detail of her education and her experience. It was like you pulled a string on her back and out came her résumé. I immediately thought of that Barenaked Ladies song: "Anyone perfect must be lying..."

Soon we reached the cube where Isabella would be incarcerated on a daily basis and maybe even profiled on one of those MSNBC prison shows. I mean, she would be brought there at six months and wouldn't even be able to crawl yet, so would it matter? The main selling point was that it was near Audge's work, and she would be close by and could check on her. We kept telling ourselves this to make ourselves feel better because we were starting to feel uneasy.

But then it got worse. If you see any of these things at a daycare you're looking at, *leave immediately*. Like if you're in a haunted house and the walls start bleeding. Don't go upstairs to see what's in the attic. Just freaking leave. First of all, there were TODDLERS in her room. The babies were mixed in with the toddlers! There were actually babies on the floor and toddlers running around. I couldn't believe my eyes. Now, at the time I didn't know that much about daycare but I did know that young children should be separated by age and care requirements. I mean, you're supposed to do that with everything from tropical fish to kittens, right? You wouldn't toss tropical fish in with kittens, would you? Sure, they had a "gated area" for the babies for alone time, but it didn't look like much fun. One of the babies inside was playing a harmonica and trying to put up a poster of Rita Hayworth.

The next red flag was the caregivers themselves. They all looked miserable. They weren't enjoying their jobs. I mean, I wasn't expecting a smile from a vintage USO poster, but still. These women didn't smile at all. It's not like they were welding aircraft carriers together either. I know child care is hard work, but here's an idea: *Hire some people who actually want to do it*. At that point my initial ignorance of daycare facilities was being replaced by the feeling that something was definitely not right here.

As we continued to look around and take it all in, we saw some of the older kids eating at a small table. They were maybe between twelve and eighteen months. One child dumped his food on the floor and the "caregiver" took the rest of the food away and annoyingly said to the child, "I guess you're done." At that point, so was I.

Then the coup de grâce. A baby was crying on the floor. Soon it became a wail. No one moved. No one was going to comfort this child. None of the caregivers even seemed concerned about it. They were preoccupied with other children. Finally my mother-in-law said what I was thinking to our tour guide: "How long are you going to let that baby cry?" Our tour guide politely answered that all of the other caregivers were busy, and that the baby would have to wait. She said it teaches them patience. What?! Yes, because that's what all six-month-olds need to learn: patience. What the hell was wrong with this woman? My wife and I wanted to shove her face into the Diaper Genie. She started the tour by telling us how qualified she was, all this previous employment in child care, all her education, etc. Hiding incompetence behind a degree. What a novel concept. Thank God no one in our government does that.

Looking back, I can't believe what I heard. But at the

time I was taking it all in with no frame of reference. Even so, I knew that something was wrong. Finally a caregiver went and picked up the poor crying child. She did it mechanically, which got me a little excited because I thought, "Well, maybe she's a robot," but it turned out she was just disinterested and apathetic.

The "tour" was nearing its conclusion but by then I really didn't want to hear another word this woman had to say. Now when she talked all I heard was Darth Vader's theme by John Williams. We left in stunned silence. I thought to myself I would never send my child for daycare here but if I wanted her to do hard time I might think about it.

On the very uncomfortable car ride home we kept saying, "Is that what daycare is really like?" All of Audge's work friends raved about the place. Maybe they never actually saw it or perhaps every tenth room is run differently, with happy caregivers. I didn't want to bring my child there and neither did Audge. But could we find another daycare and get through the waiting list in time? Thankfully, we got lucky. For real this time.

A friend of mine suggested we check out her daycare. It was a much smaller facility and had a lot of other interesting programs and perks. So we scheduled another tour. The difference was immediate. It was smaller, open, bright, and friendly. Our tour guide didn't try so hard to impress us because the place spoke for itself. The caregivers looked happy and friendly. One even smiled, saluted, and said she had just come from welding an aircraft carrier together. OK, maybe I was projecting. But it was clear they actually enjoyed their work. We entered the infant room where Isabella would be and saw there were *just* infants in there. No toddlers. Wow, what a great idea.

The room was quiet and bright. Not many kids, and none of them were crying. But then one started to and the caregivers all had their hands full with changing and feeding. As one of the actually concerned caregivers tried to quickly finish up a diaper change to get to the crying child, our tour guide said, "Excuse me," washed her hands, stepped in, and comforted the child. Night and day. These people actually *cared* about children. We were sold and we both breathed a huge sigh of relief. We had a daycare for Isabella. And our friend got a free month as a referral bonus! She said she spent the money she saved on donuts and vodka. Good for her.

Our daycare has a very interesting program. They have a daycare and a senior center next to each other and every day the children interact with the seniors, or the "neighbors," as they call them. Here in LA it looks like the Friars Club meets *Romper Room*. In fact, it is such a unique program that it got nationwide attention and was profiled on both local and national news. At one year old

Isabella was on *Good Morning America*. She now had her first TV credit.

But there were a lot of other things we had to consider when choosing a daycare, other than beefing up our infant's television résumé. The first, most important thing you should look for is finding someone who actually wants to take care of your child. I'd say that should be obvious, but after our first experience I'm not so sure it is. Like the sign that says "Do Not Touch the Electric Fence. It's Electrified."

But we found out there's a lot more to ask about. Impress your wife and pretend you came up with some of these questions on your own: Does your daycare have an open door policy? Can you go and visit anytime you want? Can you call anytime to check on your child? How is the security? Are the doors locked with keypad locks? Do you have time-traveling robots or are you at least working on them? What if there's an earthquake? (Seriously, how do they react in case of a natural disaster?) What if we are running late, will someone stay for a ridiculously large sum of penalty money? (That answer is usually yes.)

Now there is one BIG drawback to daycare as my wife and I unfortunately learned. Up at the top of this chapter I mentioned being sick all the time. When you have children in daycare, not only are they sick, but they bring every germ imaginable back into your home faster and more often than social workers into Britney Spears's house. Not normal germs, we're talking *Andromeda Strain* stuff. It's Germ Warfare. That's the only way I can accurately describe it. You want to decimate an enemy army? Just open up a daycare center behind enemy lines. Soon half the enemy army will be throwing up and the other half will be shivering from some type of new flu virus that evolved from infants putting blocks in their mouths.

Isabella would come home with some new germ and within a few days my wife and I would get it. Not just colds, mind you. Oh, no. Nice, violent intestinal bugs, weird conjunctiveitis-y goo coming out the eyes, and occasionally a kidney stone. OK, maybe I can't blame that one on daycare, but I'm not completely convinced. At one point it honestly felt like we were paying a monthly fee for the privilege of having never-ending dry heaves. The good news is that after you live for a year in the daycare "hot zone," your infant's immunities will reboot and she will get less sick. And, thankfully, so will you. But man, that is one long year. During this time the next person who looks at your infant and says, "The time goes by so fast," you have my permission to punch them in the eye. Or better yet, sneeze on them.

Now, as much as we liked our facility, when everyone was healthy anyway, no daycare is perfect. There may be a problem every once in a while with care, a new caregiver, a new policy, a giant ant infestation, new hours, a transition to a new room, etc. So another really good thing to do is talk to the facility director. Are they accessible? Will they respond positively and constructively if there is a concern or a problem? Or are they like the Once-ler from *The Lorax*? Are they willing to help you or just sell you a Thneed?

So you have to take everything into consideration. It's a package deal. Ultimately, it's about whether your child is getting good care and being stimulated and challenged without the use of a television screen. It's a comfort zone. You, your wife, and child ALL have to be comfortable where you are, or it won't work out.

But the most important thing: No matter what you hear about a facility or school, good or bad, you HAVE to go check it out for yourself. Remember, this is your child. Why would you go on secondhand information? We learned that lesson. I'm trying to save you some time. I don't care if the ratio is eight caregivers per child and the rooms are made of gold. See for yourself. And if the facility is run by time-traveling robots, then sign up immediately.

16

I See a New Mother, but Where the Hell Did My Wife Go?

Out of all the adjustment stuff that made me crazy, I have to say this one was one of the hardest things and one I didn't see coming. I expected all of the mood swings and hormonal shifts going up and down even after the birth, but there were a few unwanted hitchhikers on that ride, like a complete aversion to sex and a resentment about my concern about the complete aversion to sex.

My wife just didn't want to have sex anymore, even months after the birth, which was a C-section, so it's not like anything even got messed with down there. It was just a string of curt excuses. At first it was the pregnancy, then it was the delivery, then it was exhaustion. Then it was because *Grey's Anatomy* was on. I didn't know what was going on. Was it hormonal? It was as if a weird switch went off in my wife's brain. She was thinking, "We originally had sex to practice making a baby. Now I have a baby. So why would I ever want to have sex again? I'm done with that."

My wife would get angry if I would even suggest sex. She had absolutely no sex drive. I thought it was a phase and I rode it out. It wasn't. I felt like I was stuck in a very G-rated *Groundhog Day*. I would get up in the morning and think: Is this still the day I don't have sex? It wasn't getting any better and finally we had a "discussion."

I was trying to get to the root of the problem, mainly because I wanted to make sure it wasn't me. Finally I said, "Father Tony said we should never withhold sex from each other." Father Tony was my cousin and the priest who married us. Catholics have this whole premarriage ritual involving classes, donations, and guilt before you get married. At the time I thought it was weird getting sex advice from a priest, but it was much weirder bringing up said priest sex advice in an argument.

Now we're both pretty easygoing and stubborn at the same time. On paper, that works out beautifully. When one of us is being stubborn, the other one is being easygoing and vice versa. But occasionally we're out of sync. This was one of those times. I don't know if the priest advice was the tipping point or I had just worn her out, but finally my wife agreed to talk to the doctor about it, only after I threatened to talk to the doctor about it myself.

Now I didn't really think there was anything wrong with her that pharmaceutical science couldn't cure. Surely they had a sex pill by now, right? Some kind of legal roofie? Turns out, they did. Her doctor said it was perfectly normal for a woman to lose her sex drive for months after the birth. Excuse me, *many* months? Her doctor prescribed hormone therapy.

But he prescribed testosterone. Freaking testosterone!? OK, so it was a few weeks' worth of treatment and I had to bug her to take the pill and have sex so ultimately it ended up being more work for me. She claimed it didn't make a difference but I noticed a difference right away. She was getting . . . less angry about it. But then the pills ran out and she didn't want to take them anymore. I was worried about side effects of testosterone therapy but I don't think there were any. I just can't talk to her when the game is on and she can now bench over 600 pounds.

Finally, things started to get better. Audge got less angry about sex, but we had to schedule it and when we did do it, it was a bit . . . mechanical. But hey, by then I didn't even fucking care. At least I was getting some. Eventually things did normalize but it took a *long* time. Over a year. Every woman is different and I wish you Godspeed. Truly.

Now keep in mind her hormones are still going crazy,

even if she's not adding to the mix in pill form. But this part, I got. I knew my wife's body was trying to return to normal and that there would be some, well, malfunctions along the way.

My wife would start crying sometimes, even when I didn't do anything. Then the floodgates would open at random: "Why did we wait so long to have a child? It's your fault. Why don't you like changing diapers?! She's your *child*! Why do I have to do everything around here?! I'm still recovering from the surgery *and* taking care of the baby. . . ." There was so much and it was such a blur I suddenly felt like I was getting yelled at by Willy Wonka. "I, the undersigned, shall forfeit all rights, privileges, and licenses herein and herein contained, et cetera, et cetera . . . Fax mentis incendium gloria cultum, et cetera, et cetera . . . Memo bis punitor delicatum! . . . Good day, sir!"

At this point you really have to think of your wife as an overheated radiator. If you try to reason with an overheated radiator by pouring cold water on it, it will explode. But if you leave it alone and let it vent until it runs out of steam, you'll find it much easier to deal with. So don't engage. Just nod and think about sports, or if buying a Blu-ray DVD player is really worth it while she tells you how you're always emptying the dishwasher incorrectly. Evasive action, Mr. Sulu!

One thing you should keep an eye out for at this time is a thing called postpartum depression. My wife didn't have it. She was on the opposite end of the spectrum like the baby was some kind of high for her. She was more postpartum elation. But I say this because it's important and some women do get it.

Look for the warning signs of postpartum depression. They are . . . well . . . depression. It's actually right there in the title. It's not that hard to spot and alert your doctor if you notice it.

Home Sweet Work

So now we've gone through the physical and emotional changes, what about the practical ones? It's amazing how my wife and I can have vastly different perceptions on something as simple as how to spend a weekend. It often begins with her saying, "Are you just going to sit there all day?" Apparently not. The weekend is no time for relaxing. Get up! There's work to be done!

My wife once went out on a Saturday, took Isabella, and left me a list of things to do. As you know, when you get a list of things to do, there is always that subtle undertone of "this better be done before I get back." I heard it loud and clear. So, I actually did everything on the list. Now I usually don't do one or two things on a list to make it look like some of the other things took a long time. This way I can get some Play-Station time in and still look like I was working pretty hard.

But no, not this time. This time I did everything. And

when my wife came back, she was *still* pissed. I said, "Why are you angry? I did everything on the list."

"Yes, but you don't *look* for stuff to do," she replied. I was stunned. I'm a guy. We don't *look* for stuff to do. That would be like the Road Runner *looking* for Wile E. Coyote. It makes no sense. We men spend our whole lives trying to get out of stuff to do. What does she think we do at work all day?

That's why half the time on the weekends we have to avoid eye contact with our wives. As soon as they see us, they make us do stuff. They're like those laser guided alarms from heist movies. As soon as you break the beam, you're done. The work police have caught you. "There you are. What are you doing lying down in the closet? Anyway, get up. I have some incredibly annoying and mundane tasks for you to do immediately. And get dressed."

When you have children, there is always something to be done. It could be shopping, cleaning, fixing something, running errands, or apologizing to the neighbors for what happened the weekend before. When you have children *and* a house, there is something to be done every four minutes. The thing is, you are *never* going to get everything done. You just aren't. Sorry. So how do you balance everything? Good question.

My wife and I were in a routine where we would work on the house or do other work or take care of Isabella all weekend. Then back to work during the week. We were both tired and miserable and finally realized it was our own fault. The harder we tried to get everything done that needed to be done, the more miserable we became. It was like Sisyphus rolling the boulder up a hill and then watching it roll down again as soon as he was done. But instead of a boulder up a hill, it was a cart down the aisles of Home Depot.

So, we made a deal. No matter how much work there was to do, only *one* day per weekend was to be used for work. The other we go on a family outing or just relax and have fun. All of a sudden, we were feeling much better about everything. We were actually enjoying our weekends together. Imagine that. So the lesson is, everything in moderation. Even work. Actually, especially work.

Your relationship with your wife will be completely different from now on. Your new baby is kind of an X Factor and it will take some time for both of you to adjust. All you've known together is two. Now there's three.

But you have to take time for each other, and alone time. When family comes over, go out like a couple. Go on a date. Or find a trustworthy babysitter. You simply have to do it or your marriage will suffer. Remember why you got married in the first place, other than your wife pressuring you into it. Just because you have a baby doesn't mean you're not still husband and wife.

Like I said, it took my wife a *long* time to adjust to this. "We can have a date here at home" was the unhelpful suggestion she would make and obviously was missing the point completely. On top of everything else, my wife was having a bit of separation anxiety and didn't want to leave the baby with anyone but my mother, her mother, or as a last resort, me. Since we only saw our mothers a few times a year, that meant we had "date night" only once every three to four months. Like everything else, it got better and we reached the babysitter stage but again, it takes a while.

This can be a tough adjustment for you both and you have to keep the lines of communication and the wine bottles open. You're simply going to see some things very differently. "I think we should go out to dinner and maybe see a movie."

"Why?"

"Because . . . I didn't think you were going to say *that* . . . because . . . it's . . . a cultural ritual ingrained into my heritage as a consumer."

"Your mother's coming to visit in four months. We'll go out then."

This is a time that will require you to be patient as well as supportive. Now let's bring back some pregnancy advice that applies here as well: Every once in a while keep your mouth shut. Once my wife said, "I miss the body I had when I was twenty-two." Apparently the correct response is *not* "so do I."

17

Pediatricians, Vaccines, and Celebrities

You don't just "find" a pediatrician when you have a child. No, there is an interview process that seemingly entails background checks, charts, graphs, and even high school references. And it starts early. When she was about six months pregnant, my wife came home from work one day and said we were falling behind on our pre-parental duties. My first question was, "OK, so what kind of questions *do* we ask a pediatrician?"

My resourceful wife came back with a nice long list of questions found on the Internet. And I have to say that most were pretty obvious, like, "What are your emergency and after hours policies? Are other doctors available in your group? What are your philosophies on breastfeeding? Have you ever been convicted of a felony?" etc. There were a few less obvious ones, like, "Do you charge for phone calls?" I have never heard of a doctor charging for phone calls, but if it's on the Internet, chances are at some point someone got charged for a phone call, got angry, and made a blog post. So as you're talking to prospective pediatricians, see if they have timers next to their phones.

The easiest way to find a pediatrician is to ask someone you know who lives close to you and is happy with their doctor. We asked our neighbor, got an enthusiastic referral, and then set up our "interview."

So there we were in the kid doctor's office with no kid. I half expected the receptionist to say to us, "You're a bit early. Please come back in three months." It's hard not to feel conspicuous sitting in the waiting room with other parents with children actually sitting outside of their mother's wombs. But apparently, according to everyone's reaction, or nonreaction, I should say, it's perfectly normal and a common practice. I was the only one uncomfortable with it. As usual. That happens to me a lot.

Luckily we didn't have to wait long before we were led to the examining room. Then my wife told me to put my shirt back on and I remembered why we were there. The doctor came in and she was warm and friendly. She had done this a million times before.

My wife asked questions her friends and the Internet told her to ask. All of the answers seemed satisfactory to both of us, and we both really liked this doctor. Mainly, we felt *comfortable* with her. I think this is important. If your doctor is a genius but off-putting, who wants to be around that? It would be like hanging out with Quentin Tarantino.

We liked the doctor. First go, a success. So now what? We interview two more and pick the best one? Are we shopping for a car? We didn't have the time or energy to play infant-doctor matchmaker. We made a command decision. She wins. We had our doctor after one interview. And I think the pediatricians know that. They recognize you're only really going to have the energy for one interview so they make a good impression and know you'll be back. Well played, pediatrician. Well played indeed.

Should I get my baby vaccinated? And why is Jenny McCarthy making my wife miserable?

There used to be an easy, no-brainer answer. Should I get my baby vaccinated? Yes. Get your baby vaccinated unless you're a hillbilly or a hippie. In fact, you should definitely get your child vaccinated in case hillbillies or hippies move in next door.

But not anymore. Now it's complicated. For us, it all started with my wife's mother calling in a panic and saying, "You shouldn't get your child vaccinated. Jenny McCarthy was just on *Oprah* saying vaccines cause autism." Now, there are about a hundred things wrong with that above statement, on both the literal and even the subtextual level if you bring in Marshall McLuhan's whole "medium is the message" thing. It's one of those things that you hear but your brain doesn't really process right away. The response is always "*What?!*"

My wife's mother and sister were making her crazy about the rise in autism and the vaccines link and kept saying, "Go to Jenny McCarthy's website." For the love of God, are any solutions to *anything* ever found on a celebrity's website? Unless I'm trying to dry out or avoid the paparazzi, they have nothing to teach me.

So we did what clear, rational, thinking people do. We talked to our doctors about it. And they all said the exact same thing, and in different locations. They didn't even know each other. To paraphrase, this is what they said: "There is no medical evidence to link autism with vaccines. The problem is that celebrities with no medical knowledge go on talk shows and spread inaccurate information."

Wait a minute, are you saying Jenny McCarthy, from MTV's *Singled Out*, has no medical background? My whole worldview has just been thrown off kilter. But in the interest of ironic full disclosure, I was actually a freelance writer for *Singled Out* so I suppose we have that in common. Not that either one of us is bragging about it. And no, I don't know her personally. I met her briefly at a wrap party and that was it but I still talk to former host Chris Hardwick on occasion, in case you were wondering. Actually, I'm pretty sure you weren't.

So the doctors all agreed, saying vaccines don't cause autism and it's not something we should be worried about. If people stopped vaccinating their children, these diseases would come back into society, especially if there was some kind of environmental disaster. Then it would be too late. If that happened we'd all be quite busy trying to avoid the hungry giant cockroaches that would jump to the top of the food chain. That would leave very little time to find a clinic with a rubella vaccine.

Now, I am not saying for *one second* you should trust completely and implicitly pharmaceutical companies with a lot of money at stake or incompetent, bureaucratic government agencies who are supposed to regulate them. But I did trust our doctors. We picked them to have our child's well-being in mind, and they simply know more about medicine than we do. So we trusted their opinions. They were up on recent studies and were aware of the controversy.

But eventually I got dragged into the family fray. My mother-in-law said, "What about *Lorenzo's Oil*? Those doctors don't know what they're talking about." I have to admit she had a point. And she used a movie reference to do it, so I was impressed.

Unfortunately, that still didn't help me. The problem is that no one really knows for sure what's causing the rise in autism, so in theory it could still be anything, including hereditary factors, environmental exposure, the age of the father (the higher the age, the greater the autism risk), better and earlier diagnosis of autism, even some combination of those factors and/or vaccines that has yet to be discovered. So my choices were: listen to my doctors (good), listen to an ex–*Playboy* Playmate (bad), or build my own lab and find out what's causing the rise in autism myself (too much work).

Ultimately we listened to our pediatrician, who was going to medical school while Jenny McCarthy was . . . enjoying herself . . . at the Playboy Mansion. We did get full vaccinations for our child. Now, I do think the doctors try to give too many at once so we spread them out a bit and watched very closely for side effects and anything out of the ordinary. My wife and I felt the small risk of the unknown was much less than the risk of our child actually getting any of these fatal diseases.

So did we feel comfortable getting Isabella vaccinated?

Absolutely. Still not sure about it? Call your doctor. As long as they don't have a timer next to the phone.

THINGS YOU DON'T WANT TO HEAR WHEN INTERVIEWING A PROSPECTIVE PEDIATRICIAN

1. "Sorry I'm late. Man, I did want to make a good impression on my first day."
2. "I'm on vacation a lot and I don't like cell phones."
3. "I'm sorry you had to hear that. My husband is such an asshole. So, are you having a boy or a girl?"
4. "Sorry for keeping you in the waiting room for so long. Tell you what, I'll give you a free vaccine. Your choice."
5. "To be honest, I really wanted to be a veterinarian."
6. "Are you going to be breastfeeding? Good. If you have any left over, let me know."
7. "If you can find a cheaper doctor than me, good luck."
8. "Not that it matters, but I like to know: Are you a Republican or a Democrat?"
9. "I like to think of myself as more of a guidance counselor than a doctor."
10. "I'll tell ya, I am *so* glad I don't have kids."

18

Babyproofing, Safety, and Tilting at Windmills

I didn't want to believe it. They're so little. How much trouble can they cause? Now I'm sure the Romans once said that about the Huns. One thing I learned about babies: small but mighty. Sure, you can babyproof. You can even pay someone hundreds of dollars to do it for you. So you think you're safe, right? Wrong. You need to think of your child as if you were in the movie *Jurassic Park*. "Life will find a way." No matter how much you babyproof, how much you think you've thought of everything, it doesn't matter. The baby velociraptor will still find a way into the cabinet with the most breakables.

Now, I expected Isabella to be destructive, sure. I expected her to throw her bottle from the high chair. What I didn't expect was that she would have perfect aim and throw the bottle right into the cat's ceramic food dish just after it had been filled, sending milk, ceramic pieces, and Fancy Feast all over the kitchen. It can't be deliberate. Can it?

The fact is, babies are a lot stronger than they look. They put their whole bodies into whatever they do. Again, small but mighty. Remember that scene in the first *Superman* movie where baby Clark lifted the truck while John Kent was changing the tire? Let's just say a lot of emergency room visits are preceded by the sentence: "It's OK, he's not strong enough to—Oh, my God!"

The good news is if you pay attention, eventually you will be able to anticipate accidents. Once Isabella wound up her arm like a New York Yankees pitcher with a full sippy cup gripped in her hand. And she was aiming at our beautiful 50-inch plasma TV. I swear everything went into slow motion at that point. I was in a Michael Bay movie, yelling, "Nooooooo!" as the villain with long greasy hair and a goatee pressed the detonator. I yelled so loudly that it took Isabella by surprise, giving me a chance to get over there and disarm her. I then quietly and soothingly said, "It's OK, everything's OK." I was talking to the television.

Accidents can happen at any time and will often happen at home. Usually when you least expect them. That's why they're called accidents and not "predictable and scheduled misfortunes."

One night I was in the kitchen and my wife had taken our daughter into the bedroom. A few moments later I heard a crash and two screams. Isabella had fallen off the bed and hit her head on our nightstand. A huge welt was already starting to form. Isabella was still screaming and my wife was starting to look panicked. I was worried as well. When things like this happen, don't debate what to do. Just get in the car and go to the hospital or urgent care center. You don't fuck around with head injuries. Just go.

We took Isabella immediately to the pediatric urgent care center. Which, by the way, you should always know *in advance* where it is. Seriously, take a dry run or have the MapQuest page by the door. Our pediatric urgent care facility was right above our pediatrician's office so we knew where it was.

On the ride over Audge felt so bad this had happened on her watch and kind of guessed I was upset with her too. Now, I'll admit that wasn't really fair. Accidents are accidents and sometimes they are going to happen no matter how careful you are. Be supportive and then when it happens to you, you can mention how supportive you were when it happened to her. That's right, put that little chip aside for a rainy day.

At urgent care, the doctor examined Isabella and ordered an X-ray but he didn't seem too worried. He reassured us that bumps on the head usually look much worse than they are. He asked if she screamed right away and I said yes but I wasn't sure what my wife's reaction had to do with anything. Then he clarified and asked if our *daughter* cried right away. Yes. Her too. He informed us if your child hits his or her head and *doesn't* cry right away, it may be more serious. Good to know for the future.

After examinations and X-rays it turns out all Isabella had was a bad bump on the head, which was a huge relief. It's a horrible feeling when your child gets hurt. You feel a mixture of severe guilt and sorrow and run over in your head a thousand ways it could have been prevented. Big plastic bubbles come to mind. Of course, none of that does you any good now.

The incident sparked a theory of mine. What I'm about to tell you is confidential. Don't bring this up to any woman ever. They will deny it and get angry at you for suggesting it. This is an interesting phenomenon and I checked this with a few of my male friends. *Your child is more prone to accidents with your wife than with you.* The obvious question is why? Or why would I even mention this and risk an *Oprah* boycott? The reason has to do with, ironically, something women are inherently better at than men: multitasking. Good for the office, bad for child care.

I'm lucky if I can concentrate on one thing at a time. Right now, as I'm writing, I'm thinking about chicken parmesan, for no reason. So it's tough for us to do one thing, let alone many. Stay with me here. Since men are not good at multitasking to begin with, when we are watching a child, we *never* multitask because we are so overwhelmed by that one job that it gets our whole, nervous, undivided attention.

So why were we at urgent care with Isabella? Because my wife put our daughter on the middle of the bed and then tried to get changed. She was trying to do many things at once. Multitasking. Or trying to. Again, we men suffer from no such compulsion. One thing at a time, if that, is the way we do things and we're sticking to it. Or if you're a guy working on a road crew, then it's one thing every six days or so and the rest of the time you rearrange orange cones or hold up a sign. No need to rush anything; it's just a road.

If you see your wife trying to do too many things at once, stop her. Do it for the safety of your child. Of course, you could actually help out more and do one of the things that she's trying to do, so she won't have a reason to multitask, but I'll leave that to your discretion.

Look, safety is a *huge* issue for infants and toddlers. It can't be taken too seriously. They have no threat assessment and it is your responsibility to keep them safe. In fact, if anything, they have a reverse threat assessment. A threat *encouragement*.

When visiting one of the grandparents, they had the dishwasher open and as soon as they turned away Isabella had a knife in her hand. And the car keys. Like she had been planning something and was just waiting for her chance. You can't turn your back for a second. I swear they sense it. As soon as all eyes are elsewhere, a bell goes off in their heads. Ding Ding! "Now's my chance. I'm going to grab or do something dangerous to myself, others, or the pet, in an order yet to be determined."

And remember, just because your house is baby-proofed (or so you think) doesn't mean anyone else's is. Keep this in mind when you visit other homes and especially when you visit the grandparents. There hasn't been a small child in their house for quite some time so there will be plenty of things that need a good breaking within easy reach. Remember, visiting toddlers are like miniature coked-up, eighteenth-century gold miners and a new house is like California to them.

Your level of comfort with your child's safety will be different from that of other parents. I think that is fine since all children are different. You can adjust your parenting to your child's risk and danger proclivity. If you have a short little daredevil, buy extra helmets, knee pads, elbow pads, and tranquilizers. If you have a Nervous Nelly who likes being inside all day, buy him a skateboard. Strike a balance.

The concept of "pre-worrying" about things will often creep into your thoughts and frankly is an inevitable parental right. Everything from the perils of dating to nuclear annihilation will cross your mind in every possible scenario (i.e., how will dating be different after a nuclear apocalypse) as you think about how it will affect your eight-month-old.

One of the things I'm "pre-worrying" about has to do with safety and exposure to harmful media. Nowadays there is way more stuff to keep your kids away from than when we were kids, from music with explicit lyrics to violent video games. Cable and prime-time shows are full of sex and violence and boring, contrived writing but that's another story. Of course, you have to worry about the Internet now too. You even have to watch what sites your kids are looking at and who they're talking to. Geez.

Mediawise, it seems like our parents had a lot less to worry about. Our parents never had to worry about an Eminem CD lying around and accidentally being played. My mother left her *entire* collection of John Denver albums right in the cabinet. They were just lying there without any type of lock whatsoever! I remember as a child sneaking into the cabinet when she wasn't looking and . . . not playing them.

19

Children's Programming or Programming Children?

I confess, I have a love/hate relationship with our television. How much more could I get done if it wasn't there, and maybe how much smarter I would be, but oh, how it comforts and soothes me with its warm, radiating goodness.

But now that I have a child, I want to be more aware of how it's used, and how it can be abused. The last thing I would ever want is a child who's sitting in front of the television for hours a day as her brain is being slowly turned to paste. Everyone knows television isn't good for children, but how bad is it? Turns out, for kids under two, pretty bad.

So my advice is succinct and to the point: Turn off the television. Do it right now. But why the sudden backlash against the magic friend box? Because we're becoming more aware of its effect on young minds. The American Academy of Pediatrics (www.aap.org) recommends no screen media for children under two. Why? Because television and other screen media have images that appear too rapidly for a child's brain to process, and can "short circuit" the brain development and possibly lead to ADD and attention problems later on. It creates too much unnatural stimulation for a child's brain. Personally, I think this makes perfect sense.

That's right, I'm getting all research with this chapter, but I think it's important. I think it's necessary because you're going to find someone who will disagree and think it's crazy. There are morons who will argue with you and dispute these studies and say all of the pediatricians are wrong along with all of the other organizations that say the same thing, like the Learning Disabilities Association of America (www.ldaamerica.org).

But is it really even possible to keep your child away from the television for two years? No, I don't think it is. But be smart about it. They don't even move around much that first year. You can watch it, just face your child away from it. They may try and move their heads to see, so put them in one of those restraining "bouncy" chairs that they have and block it. No big deal. If that doesn't work, then tape *Lost* and watch it when she is asleep. I wouldn't recommend watching anything horrible with your infant in the room either. Their hearing is very acute. Keep *Saw* off the TV with your child in the room. We can play *Grand Theft Auto* later too.

We managed to keep our child away from the television almost completely for the first year. And it's really not that hard. Of course, our parents thought we were crazy, and Audge's mom let her know she was plopped in front of the television for large amounts of time and she turned out fine. I agreed because I obviously had no choice, but it doesn't mean that the risk wasn't there. And it doesn't matter what our parents chose *then*. Our house, our rules, for children and for parents.

I will say my father didn't believe me when I told him about TV's effect but later caught a news story that said the same thing and now believes it. So he didn't believe what we said about television until the television told him it was true.

I got into an argument about this with one of my relative's loony friends. She said there is *no* evidence to support television has any harmful effects on children. I tried to tell her that there have been *a lot* of studies and the

American Academy of Pediatrics along with the Learning Disabilities Association of America all recommend no television for children under two. Here is the finding of one of the studies:

> *A recent research study led by Dr. Dimitri Christakis looked at the connection between the amount of television that very young children watch and attention problems years later when those children are in school. Parents were asked about how much television their children watched each day at ages one and three. When those children were about seven years old, parents were asked about how well their child was able to pay attention, how well he or she was able to focus, whether they were impulsive and easily distractible. Dr. Christakis and his team found that for each additional hour of television they watched on average before age three, they were 10 percent more likely to have attentional problems by their parents' report.* [*]

But this woman would hear none of it. So finally, I just gave up and stopped talking. You can't argue with closed-minded morons. Believe me, I've tried. Remember, I've worked in the entertainment industry.

---

[*] Christakis, Dimitri A., Frederick J. Zimmerman, Davie L. DiGiuseppe, and Carolyn A. McCarty, "Early Television Exposure and Subsequent Attentional Problems in Children," *Pediatrics* 113 (2004):708–713.

So did we show our daughter DVDs and videos? Yes, but after the first year. At that point we introduced DVDs and videos on a very limited basis. She freaking *loved* them. From *Baby Einstein* to *Sesame Street*, she was hooked. It was like video crack for her. So it only became more evident how easy it is to get hypnotized by pretty, colorful, flashing images. At least that's what my wife says every time I turn on the PlayStation.

DVDs and videos are great when your baby is sick, when you need to calm them down, or you both just need a little quiet time. Isabella used to get a lot of ear infections and the pain would really cause her a lot of discomfort. But when I popped in a Baby Einstein DVD, the program distracted her from her earache.

So I think limited exposure to media between one and two years old isn't too horrible and can actually be comforting and soothing. I honestly don't think DVDs on a *limited* basis from age one to two will negatively impact your child's brain development. Of course, if you can make it zero TV watching, then you are my hero.

Thanks to basic cable there are now hundreds of shows out there. How can you tell what's good and what isn't? There are many greedy people out there who dress in silly costumes and sing horrible songs who are all trying to hook your child and then separate you from your money. Actually, it's not that hard. The good stuff is really good, and the bad stuff is really horrible.

Sesame Street is a good cause and they can actually give Disney a run for their money when it comes to marketing. Elmo is their god. His name is easy to say and instantly addictive. One of Isabella's first words was "Elmo." In *Sesame Street*'s defense, their videos are not only engaging, but they are always educational, fun, and watchable for adults. I recommend them, even with Elmo, who is just as annoying as you remember him.

The same goes for Barney. I did a bit of a turnaround on Barney. He's not nearly as annoying as I remembered, but still pretty annoying. Still, our daughter loves him and he does teach as he entertains. However, his little dinosaur minions creep me out. Barney has these two kid dinosaurs—BJ and Baby Bop—with him and they are *unbelievably* annoying. You just want them to be hit with a huge comet so they can become extinct all over again. And they are supposed to be brother and sister but if you look at them, they are different species of dinosaur. What the hell?! One's a triceratops and the other is a brachiosaurus or something. Where's the backstory?! Still, all in all, Barney isn't too bad.

Now, the Wiggles fucking suck. There. I said it. With no lessons, education, or redeeming value, the Wiggles, like many others, are essentially junk food for your child's brain. And babies and toddlers freaking *love* them. They come out in their fake *Star Trek* shirts, pretend to play instruments, and bring out the cheapest, sloppiest costumes you have ever seen. Let's see, an octopus, a dinosaur, a dog, and a gay pirate with a feather for a sword. What?! But to your kid, it makes perfect sense. Isabella loved the Wiggles.

I did find a kids' band that I actually really liked. Check out Dan Zanes and Friends. Imagine if real musicians actually sang songs for your children. Dan's from the Del Fuegos. Remember them? At the time you probably had big hair and were wearing parachute pants. And so was your wife. Dan and his band are fun to listen to, and their videos are fun to watch. Their CDs also feature a few other actual musicians like Sheryl Crow. But the main thing is it's not junk food for your child's brain. These are actual artists making music and do not talk down to children. Unlike adults, children know when they are being patronized, whether it's from a grown-up or an entertainer. They don't like it. Thankfully, Isabella had outgrown the Wiggles at around two.

Unfortunately, the Disney Channel is full of lame-ass programming for young children. Thankfully, at least they show their blocks for young children commercial free. But they do advertise their other crappy shows. The problem is, Isabella loves the *Mickey Mouse Clubhouse*, the most poorly animated and poorly produced animated show on television today. Why would you do that to your most beloved character?

But I have to give them credit for demographics. Disney knows their audience, and Isabella doesn't care that Mickey's head moves independently from his ears.

PBS is so much better on every level, from the educational content to the entertainment value. They do kids' shows right. *Sesame Street, Curious George, Between the Lions,* and *Dragon Tales* are all great shows. Try to make them more available to your child than the vapid mass-produced TV schlock on basic cable. The good news is with DVRs, TiVos, and On Demand programming, a lot of these excellent shows are available at your fingertips.

But still, the best advice is to just shut the television off. As adults, it's like delatching from an electronic glowing teat. There's almost withdrawal. But when you turn off the television, a weird thing happens. You'll find you're interacting with others more. And not just with your children but with your spouse and other people as well. Turning off the light-and-noise machine forces you to acknowledge that there are other people in the room. It's uncomfortable at first, but you'll get used to it.

As you use the television both with and without your children, think about what lessons you want to impart to them about media. They say it takes a village to raise a child, but I don't think that necessarily means a global village. There is a lot more constantly coming at both us adults and our children through the medium of television, not to mention the Internet. So in addition to everything else, you now have a new job as digital gatekeeper. Welcome aboard. But when it gets to be too overwhelming, think: WWMMD? What would Marshall McLuhan do?

20

What's the Best Way to Parent?

This is one of those things that shouldn't be complicated, but it is. Or not complicated so much as obfuscated. The first thing we learned is that there are so many theories and advice on how to parent. It's insane. Back in the old days there was one way to parent. If your kid survived, you were a good parent. If not, then you weren't. End of story.

I will say this one was also partially our fault. The reason is we were so nervous about being new parents we tried to compile all the information we could from friends, neighbors, relatives, books, and the Internet. This is a huge mistake. It's not that it is too much information, which it is, the problem is that while we got some great information, the bulk of it was ultimately worthless. It only proved to make us more nervous. Which parenting technique do we pick? *The Lady or the Tiger?*

I think this is an end result of our generation being *too* worried about being parents. And the market has responded. "Worried about being parents? Then buy this. Now this. And this. Now try this. Didn't work? OK, now try this." That is unless you *want* your child to be far behind developmentally. "Buy this or you will have a stupid baby," is the marketing shorthand. Why do you think the products are called Baby Einstein and Baby Genius, and not Baby Average?

So, short of covering your eyes and ears for the next two years, you're going to hear about every single crazy parenting technique from diaperless babies to talking to them without ever using the word "no." And no, I didn't just make those two up. And yes, I just defiantly used the word no.

Rest assured, worry bells go off when you have a problem. And then what do you do? To the Internet, old chum! We experienced one of the more common problems: Isabella had a lot of trouble sleeping. For some reason she saw no need to sleep at night or for extended periods of time. She had places to go and people to wake up. Wide awake at 3:00 a.m.? That was her infant party time. "Why do you adults look so sleepy? Come on, walk me around the house. Why are you stopping to get some water? Come on, let's go!"

So we searched for solutions and found the Richard Ferber technique, or how to "Ferberize" your baby. I know, sounds like something you do to your car, but what the hell, we wanted to try something and were really, really tired.

We bought the book and tried to read it, but we were so tired it took a while to realize I had picked up a Harry Potter book by mistake. "This says we should give him gillyweed and say a spell."

"Whatever, let's try it."

Ferberizing is when you use a type of twelve-step program to get your baby to sleep and wean him off his addiction to . . . staying awake. The steps include picking him up and letting him cry in various increments until one of you falls asleep from exhaustion.

So we tried the Ferber technique on Isabella, letting her cry, picking her up, etc., on and on for a while. Here's the thing: Sometimes it worked and sometimes it didn't. So should you stay rigidly to the program? I say no, although Dr. Ferber may disagree with me. Which brings us back to the previous advice. Use all of this stuff as guidelines, not absolutes.

Your baby may be afraid of the dark, goblins, or even global warming. Whatever the reason, it's going to take patience, which unfortunately lack of sleep will put you in short supply of. Through a mixture of rocking, Ferberizing, and comforting, eventually Isabella slept through the night and got easier and easier to put down. Think of this time as a form of reverse hazing your baby is putting you through. It will take some time, but eventually you'll all sleep together comfortably at the fraternity house.

But let's just mention the granddaddy of bad parenting ideas: attachment parenting. Should you go with attachment parenting? Well, do you want a kid in his thirties who lives in your basement and never wants to leave? Except maybe to attend a Renaissance faire?

Attachment parenting is essentially having your child with you 24/7 including sleeping in your bed with you. Can you imagine anything more ridiculous? Maybe if you're trying to settle the Wild West and there are Indians and coyotes everywhere, sure, I could see having your baby with you at all times.

It makes you wonder if proponents of attachment parenting have their own issues with separation anxiety, abandonment, and severe codependency. Dr. Spock says children can sleep alone in a crib right after birth. Believe him. We kept our baby in the bassinet in our bedroom while my wife was recovering from the C-section and then moved Isabella into her own room in about six weeks. It's better for you and better for your child to have a little personal space.

Your child does not *need* you there every minute of every day. He's asleep. Let him sleep in peace. That two hours is your "break." Use it. What do you think baby monitors are for? Besides, your child needs some alone time too. If he's cooing in the crib, looking at the numerous expensive toys you've been pressured into buying, then let him enjoy his alone time. Maybe sometimes a little alone time in the playpen with a few toys is a good thing. You're still right next to them on the couch. Personal space. Everyone needs it.

Now, here comes the tricky part. Say your wife wants to try attachment parenting because one of her lunatic friends at work told her how great it is. After the baby is born, most of your conversations will end with you saying either "you're right" or "never mind." Her hormones are still going crazy, she's tired, and "you do nothing to help out around here."

Thankfully my wife saw through this attachment parenting nonsense and dismissed it as insane. But if *your* wife is insisting on trying this attachment parenting, you may have to give in at first and try it. After two days, if your wife is not convinced this is the most ridiculous idea since *Cop Rock*, you may have to say something. Seriously. There is the "fight or flight" reflex, but when dealing with new moms, the husband's reflex is usually "shut up or hide."

But you *have* to nip this in the bud. Audge's friend at work says she has a "family" bed with Mommy, Daddy, the kids, and the pets. Now, do you really want to live and sleep like a hillbilly? Of course not. Now is one of the few times you have to man up and take the heat. It will be better in the long run. No attachment parenting! Remember, detachment parenting!

But with all this parenting information overload, ultimately you have to do what my wife and I eventually did: relax a little. You have to trust your instincts and I know I've said this before, but *you know what's best for your child*. Take in the information but filter it. Think of yourself as some type of parental kidney. There is a lot of good info out there and a lot of bad. There is also a lot of bad masquerading as good but you *can* really tell the difference pretty easily. Basically, if you're reading something and you hear a cuckoo clock go off in your head, you know it's time to move on to the next website.

21

Parent Groups

They are for women. We, as men, have to draw the line *somewhere*. If you are upset that there are no Daddy and Me classes, then you are kind of like a woman and you may as well go to a Mommy and Me class. Now let us speak no more of this.

Sign, Sign, Everywhere a Sign

Every once in a while a crazy idea or trend proves to be actually correct and useful. Maybe you're familiar with baby signing or saw it first in *Meet the Fockers*. A friend of ours had raved about how great it works and after Isabella was born we asked him again what books to get. He said not to worry about it as he had gotten a book on the subject for us as a baby present. Cool!

Baby signing, which at first sounds ridiculous and new-agey, actually works. It's great and it makes your life easier. It cuts way down on your child's frustration level too, because he can communicate to you his needs without playing Twenty Questions, Infant Edition.

We started reading one of the books and learned all

about the theory, process, blah blah blah. Just tell me how does it work and what do I have to do. But then it would have been a pamphlet and not a book and publishers don't make quite as much on those.

The first thing I learned is that we had a little time before it was possible to even teach the signs. The book said children can pick up signs as early as seven months, but I doubt that. We started signing with our daughter just before her first birthday. Don't expect results right away either. It takes a bit for it to sink in. Isabella watched us sign with nothing more than a mild curiosity so we had no idea if it was sinking in or not. Turns out it was, but just keep in mind your infant will have her poker face on the whole time.

By the way, all you really need to know are two things. One: You always need to do the hand sign when you say the word like "eat," "change," or "libertarian." Two: When you say the word and do the sign, do the action it refers to all at the same time so the child can make the connection. Say "eat," do the sign for eat, and then eat. That's it, really. Wow, that would be even less than a pamphlet.

Soon after Isabella's first birthday she started gamely signing. She did basic ones and they were not exact so you have to be aware of what your child is trying to say through her rough signing. A child's signs will be crude and difficult to read, almost sloppy and intoxicated, like Jimi Hendrix if he were signing right after his set at Woodstock. For you younger readers, Woodstock was a concert held in the 1960s in New York. You know what? Never mind. I wasn't there either.

Isabella picked up on some signs, but others she couldn't care less about. She did "more" as a substitute for "eat," and ignored the "change" sign as she seemed to see no real urgency in acquiring a clean diaper.

Isabella's favorite sign soon became "more." What can I say, she likes to eat. Italian babies. It's genetically programmed. Her next sign was "all done." Then I thought how great the "all done" sign would be in other situations. We could use it with politicians, news pundits, and sitcom actors.

There are many available books and DVDs about signing. Don't get anything expensive. It's really not necessary. However, there is one DVD worth mentioning. It's a kid's signing DVD with Marlee Matlin. And she's in a really tight sweater. My wife noticed and asked if I was enjoying the DVD as much as our child. I replied, "Yes, there is something to be said for a hot deaf chick. First, she's hot, and second, when I want to get her to stop talking all I have to do is close my eyes." You would think by now my wife would not be at all shocked by anything that came out of my mouth. Judging from her expression then, it's good to see I still have the ability to surprise her. Keeps things fresh.

Anyway, at about a year and a half she started to talk more but still sign and by two she was talking and had stopped signing altogether. But I do want to note that we stopped signing too once words were being understood. My wife still gives me a few signs on occasion, but we didn't teach those to our daughter. But if you want your child to continue to use sign language as a second language, you'll need to keep using it too.

Now, there are the morons who say signing doesn't work and it will also delay your child's verbal skills, but frankly, I think that's all nonsense. You may have gotten that from my use of the word "moron." There's always going to be that fifth dentist who doesn't like Trident. While every child is different, there was no guarantee your child would have talked sooner *without* signing, so it's just another false conclusion. Like thinking if you use a different bank or airline you will actually get better service. Go ahead and think that if it makes you feel better.

So I highly recommend signing. But don't make up your own signs! It's not secret code. They use signing at daycare, and you do *not* want to confuse your one-year-old. Go with the standard American Sign Language. It will be right there in the baby signing books. Don't go looking for trouble.

But as I was teaching my daughter to sign, I realized there was a much bigger lesson here. I was showing my daughter the proper way to do things. Not telling her, but literally showing her. The lesson, for both of us, started this early by something as simple as showing her how to tell us when she was hungry. *The best way you can teach your child is by example.* This is the best advice anyone can give you about parenting and it will apply to the entirety of your children's lives. They'll see you throughout your life and will pick up on everything you say and do. Like absorbent sponges or police cameras.

23

Oh, the Places You'll Reluctantly Go: Traveling with an Infant or Toddler

I put it off as long as I could, but eventually that baby is going to have to leave the house. Since we live on the other side of the country from our families, which seems so far away, and sometimes not quite far enough, eventually we had to strap Isabella into an airplane and get her a frequent flier number.

But first things first. You can start with small trips outside the house. Stroller rides around the block or through the mall. We were typical, nervous first-time parents. We were even afraid to take our new baby to a restaurant. We didn't want to ever be "those people." You know who I'm talking about. They bring their kids to a restaurant and then the kids do nothing but scream and throw crayons and menus. Then the parents do, well, nothing. They just let the kids run around and scream and pretend they aren't even there, because obviously that's what happens at home. I never wanted to be that parent. I pictured us in a restaurant and Isabella was screaming and throwing ice cubes and trying to eat the place mat. I could hear the chant started by the other bad parents building in my head: "One of us, one of us . . ." I snapped out of my foreshadowing. Nope. Not going to happen.

But here's the crazy thing. Infants are incredibly portable. They have their own carrier, for Pete's sake. It connects to the car and fits cozily in a restaurant booth. As long as you don't go anywhere fancy, feel free to bring the wee one. Chances are he'll sleep the whole time or the restaurant will be noisy enough that no one will notice that he's fussing. If he's screaming at the top of his lungs, then yes, leave or take him outside. It's just a common courtesy. Or maybe an uncommon courtesy. Take full advantage of your porta-baby at this time. Because once they can move on their own, it's pretty much all over. As it turns out, they don't make Hannibal Lecter restraints in a toddler size.

Of course, there's always the mall. Malls during the

day are very interesting. As I was pushing Isabella in the stroller with all the other housewives and a few stray dads, I noticed it's a very different vibe in the mall during the day in the middle of the week. Everyone is calm and relaxed. It's like everyone knows this secret retreat during the day. It's quiet and not crowded. So although I've let you in on the secret of the mall, be cool and keep it to yourself, OK?

Babies *love* the mall. I would take Isabella there every time she was sick. By the way, I'm not a jerk and would never let her loose in the play area. We still don't, even when she's well. It's full of germs because a lot of parents don't care and just let their kid with bronchitis cough all over the giant plastic kangaroo. She gets enough of that in daycare, thank you very much. When she was sick, she was confined to the stroller and quite happy about it.

Sometimes taking a stroll in a mall during the day was the only thing that would calm Isabella down when she wasn't feeling well. Something about the movement, the lights, the sense of retail desperation, and the smell of deep-fried foods all made her feel better. Isabella looked around, enjoyed the ride, and often fell asleep within twenty minutes. Sometimes we would get something to eat and do our part to help keep the daytime mall economy going.

So now you know what all the other housewives

protect: The mall during the day in the middle of the week is a secret, soothing magical experience filled with gaudy yet trendy clothes, tiny jars of expensive body lotion, and the alluring yet subtly disturbing smell of Cinnabon.

But for the real fun, it's on to an airplane. First of all, avoid travel within the first three months if you can. Your child is new to the world and do you really want to subject her to an onslaught of germs right from the start? Let her software boot up a bit before you put her on a flying disease box.

If you can afford it, buy the infant or toddler his own seat. Do you really want to hold the child on your lap the whole time? It's uncomfortable and it's not the safest place in case of turbulence either. An FAA-approved car seat is the safest way to travel with your infant. Plus, if you opt for the lap-sitting option, your wife will want to "share" the holding time so you're going to be doing a fair amount of the holding, regardless of what was agreed to before you got on the airplane. Think ahead.

If you really want to make your travel easier you can even buy a convertible stroller/car seat for travel. It's called a Sit 'n' Stroll and I *highly* recommend it. You wheel your infant or toddler in the airport, the wheels fold up, and it's now your infant or toddler's seat. Then as an added bonus, when someone picks you up from the airport or you rent a car, it's now a car seat! It's like having your very own Transformer. Optimus Prime himself is helping transport your baby.

It won't be all smooth sailing. But you already knew that, right? Sometimes the hassles can come from unexpected sources. On one flight an airline flight attendant saw our Sit 'n' Stroll and started to give me lots and lots of static about it when I asked for a belt extender. Now, I held my tongue because I did not want to get thrown off the plane. But I can say to you, the reader, she was a real . . . well, let's just use the word stewarbitch. Clearly this woman had spent her whole life in a fully upright and locked position. And she was the kind of overly polite stewarbitch that masks her hatred of you and your car seat in "sirs" and fake smiles. "Sir, we have rules," etc.

You can't reason with someone like that, so don't even bother trying. Forget telling her that your car seat is FAA approved and you just need a belt extender to connect it properly. What you have to do is let her figure it out or get so frustrated she doesn't care. This is called "letting the airline stewarbitch run its course." Eventually she came back with a seat-belt extender. I gave her my verbal thanks and my silent contempt.

Hopefully your child will sleep on the plane. We would increase the chances of this by taking a red-eye flight when Isabella should be asleep anyway and then if that didn't work we would increase them again by slipping a Benadryl mickey in her milk.

Another reason you shouldn't fly with an infant unless you really have to is because their little ears are too small and don't pop the way an adult's ears do. Sometimes a pacifier or feeding will help and sometimes it won't. So they may be in pain and there's not much you can do about it except apologize to the people around you. If they have kids, they'll understand. If not, well, then they'll react the way you would have about a year and a half ago.

When you finally get to your destination, the real fun begins. When you visit the grandparents, especially the first few times, the red carpet really gets rolled out. When we visit my mother, there is new soap, towels, any type of toiletry, food, milk, and anything we need. I've been in hotels that weren't as well stocked.

You'll also be pretty much ignored, for the most part. It's now all about the baby. Audge and I looked at each other and realized we had never seen our parents so happy. This was both a compliment and an insult, I suppose. Nevertheless, Audge and I were free to then do whatever we wanted for the duration of the stay. It was "hand over that baby and please go away now."

Don't forget that unless your relatives live in Atlantis, chances are there is a store nearby where you can buy anything you may have forgotten to bring or that your relatives have refused to buy. It's helpful to have a conversation with everyone you are visiting with so you know what you need to bring or purchase when you get there. Don't assume anything. Ever.

The one thing I did notice is that when you live far away and you visit family with your new family member, you get a really high-quality visit. This happens either at your house or theirs. All the attention is on the child, and the visits take on a very special meaning. Although everyone wishes they were more frequent, when you do have the visit, it is always a special event. Saying good-bye is tough, though. Sadly, they are tear-filled events every time. It's like living through the end of *E.T.* every four to six months.

THINGS TO REMEMBER TO TAKE ON YOUR
FIRST TRIP WITH THE BABY

1. Diapers.
2. Benadryl.
3. Valium.
4. A small trash bag to hold dirty diapers and possibly anything else that may get . . . dirty.
5. Fake passports in case things really go south.
6. Change of clothes. For everyone in your row.
7. Snacks.

8. Toys.

9. Portable DVD player with two batteries. One charge for the child and one for you after he's asleep.

10. An alibi.

11. Baby wipes.

12. Doctor's phone numbers.

13. Psychiatrist's phone number.

14. Cash.

15. Cell phone.

16. Map of Costa Rica.

17. Pacifiers.

18. Adult pacifiers, shaped like small vodka bottles usually available on all flights.

19. Flare gun.

20. Guilt about living far away from your family. Actually, you don't have to pack this one. Your parents will have it waiting for you when you get there.

24

Are You a Bad Parent?

There are obvious ways to tell if you're a bad parent. If you need me to tell you to not leave your child alone in the bathtub or locked in a hot car, then you should just save everyone some time and call social services yourself right now.

But there are many different and creative ways you can be a bad parent. There's the Old Skool way, the way that miserable couples always stayed together "for the children." Because children really respond well to constant screaming and fighting in the house. Audge and I both grew up with parents who ultimately divorced or separated. It could be . . . unpleasant . . . at times. Back then we didn't really have words like "bipolar" or "manic depressive." We just had the word . . . "Italian."

And if you are in one of those unfortunate situations, for the love of God, do *not* use your children to get back at your spouse. Kim Basinger and Alec Baldwin are now the poster couple for how *not* to get divorced. Not only was their child used against each other, the family drama got played out in the national media. Wrong, wrong, wrong. Now I'm sure no one's more sorry about it than they are, except maybe their publicists. But I have to say, living in LA, it's hard to take celebrities seriously about anything. When I saw Alec Baldwin on a news special, choking up and talking about how painful his divorce was, all I could think was, "We just saw him at P.F. Chang's!"

So if you have demons (and we all do, divorced or not), keep them to yourself. They have nothing to do with your children. Leave them out of it. And if you have an actual demon, like Dr. Faustus, then please keep it away from your children as well.

But there are also new and more subtle and maybe even postmodern ways to be a bad parent. I have compiled a *partial* list of the things that really caught my attention. If you find yourself doing any of these things, please don't write me a letter telling me that I'm wrong. Just STOP. Then you'll be a good parent. Plus, you should be too busy trying to take care of your child to write me a letter.

YOU'RE A BAD PARENT IF . . .

- *Your three-year-old has a HUGE black and blue lump in the center of his forehead because he fell headfirst into some concrete stairs and you haven't called the doctor yet.*

    We dropped the parents some subtle hints at the barbecue, like "maybe you should have a doctor look at your child's head."

- *You bring your six-year-old into a 10:30 p.m. screening of* 30 Days of Night.

    Audge and I couldn't believe it. We'll see that kid in therapy later. In fact, if you're bringing a stroller into *any* movie screening after 10:00 p.m. or anything that's not rated G or PG, then you're not only a bad parent but an inconsiderate moronic prick too. And turn off your cell phone while you're at it, genius.

- *You think Las Vegas is a good place to bring your five-year-old for a "family" vacation.*

    I can't believe the amount of strollers I see in Las Vegas. GET THE BABIES OUT OF THE CASINOS! Do you really think their favorite things are smoke and noise!? And worse, I see more of them at 2:00 a.m. than ever before. Are you trying to break the record for bad parenting? Some people may argue it's a cultural thing, having kids out late at night. BULLSHIT. There are bad parents in every culture, and I've seen them; they are outside of Caesars Palace at 2:30 in the morning pushing around their crying and miserable kids in strollers.

• *You think it's funny that your two-and-a-half-year-old is destroying things in the house, and it's not your house.*

Self-explanatory, and yes, it was our house.

• *You leave your child sleeping in the car seat of your car while you go in the house because that's the only place he'll nap.*

God knows that won't traumatize him when he wakes up alone and strapped to a hot car.

• *You're protesting something, and you make your child hold up a sign.*

Your child doesn't really know what the heck abortion or gay marriage is, and doesn't care. They are only doing it to win your approval, which they are obviously not getting at home. You don't have children just to exploit them. Plus, they will resent you for it later, as they should. Now stop it.

- *You think the warning "choking hazard" on toys is just a bunch of people overreacting.*

What part of "choking" and "hazard" don't you understand?

- *If your child is screaming and you're at Disneyland.*

If your child is screaming at Disneyland, chances are it's not Disneyland that's making him scream.

While we're on the subject of Disney, my wife saw this at Disney World in Florida: We were at one of the nicer, higher-end hotels by the pool and a six-year-old girl told her mother she had to pee. Instead of taking her inside to the bathroom, which was very close, she gave her a towel, told her to wrap it around her and stand by the trash can. The mother made the daughter pee on herself in the open where people would ultimately have to walk past. My wife said the young girl peed on herself and looked ashamed and miserable. That is bad parenting on many different levels. Do I really have to say this? Do not make your children pee on themselves in public.

- *You are constantly saying to your child, "Stop crying or I'll give you something to cry about."*

Too late.

Bad parenting knows no racial, social, or economic boundaries. There are bad parents everywhere. They're easy to spot. It's not like they're hiding. Go to the mall, the park, or a restaurant, and see how many you can find. Look for the mother on the cell phone while her kid plays in the fountain.

The good news is, the converse is also true. Being a good parent has nothing to do with money, social standing, race, religion, color, or creed. I think we get way too hung up on what we can afford for our children, and not what we give them via love and attention. Oh, my wife and I got caught up in the hype too, don't get me wrong. We actually bought a baby monitor with a "pet sensor" because we were afraid our cat would jump into the crib late at night and sit on the baby's chest and steal her breath. The most the cat ever did was one day see what was actually under the crib, get bored, and walk away.

Then there's the college fund, the savings account, that gift of eleven shares of Disney stock that I have no idea what to do with, toys that teach letters, toys that teach numbers, toys that tell stories, toys that teach you how to go into massive credit card debt, etc. You know what else can teach letters and numbers and tell stories? People. That's right, you can, and you don't even have to buy batteries.

How many stuffed animals does your child actually

need? We bought some and all our relatives bought some and then our friends bought some and pretty soon we had a big hypoallergenic stuffed zoo in our daughter's room.

Really, there's just no substitute for that parent-child interaction. We found Isabella enjoyed her toys much more when we played with them with her. You're the biggest and best toy of all, sort of like in that Richard Pryor/Jackie Gleason movie.

So remember, it's not about the money you spend *on* your child, it's the time you spend *with* her that counts. Unless you spend the time with your child while you're spending your money, then that kind of cancels it out. So read books together. Play. Act childlike and goofy. Laugh together. Tell stories that make no sense, like Kurt Vonnegut.

Most important, enjoy yourself. Embrace that inner entertainer. This is the easiest audience you're ever going to have. Plus, they can't even get up and walk out of the show if you have an off night. I'm sure you'll be a smash hit. You'll find not only will you have a successful run, but you'll get held over.

25

Advice from Family and Other People, but Mostly Family

You're going to get a deluge of advice from your family on how to raise your child. It's going to come mostly from your parents, but it's also going to come from siblings, aunts, uncles, and anyone else who shares your DNA. Just so you know, everything you do regarding raising your child is going to be wrong, according to your family. Just get used to it. That's never changed in two thousand years, and it's not going to change now. Future families with children raised by robots are still going to get shit from the previous generation of robots.

On a side note, at this point you may think I am obsessed with robots. I'm really not. I'm just sure eventually they're going to take over, and I want to make a few points with them before they become our new mechanical overlords. Don't say I didn't warn you.

One of the most common pieces of advice from our parents and the previous generation when it comes to child care is to just "let them cry." The obvious question is: *Why?* Because you don't feel like getting up or you can't figure it out? Or you think an infant needs to be taught a lesson?

Now, don't get me wrong, if you have a baby with colic or other health issues, there may be nothing you can do about it. And it sucks, believe me. Colic and ear infections will keep all of you up for weeks on end. I'm not talking about that. I'm talking about if you have a healthy baby, try to figure it out. Dr. Spock says you can't spoil a child in the first six months of life. I agree with that. Attend to your child's needs. Don't "let them cry." At around six months you can start to differentiate between cries of attention and cries of need. Unless of course your baby is smarter than you. But do you really want to admit your baby is smarter than you?

We got all sorts of doozies from relatives, friends, and countless old wives tales—from feeding an infant rice cereal at two months old to putting a little whiskey on the pacifier to help them sleep. Granted, some of them were intriguing but we opted not to get our baby drunk. For now.

Now the reality is, a lot of the advice you're going to get is going to be wrong and in some cases actually harmful. We had an incident at our daycare where one of the teachers got frustrated with Isabella at the table and lightly struck her hand. Isabella didn't even react, and didn't cry, and to her it was not a big deal. Obviously it *is* a big deal if a teacher strikes a child, even lightly.

The school called and told us about the incident and let us know the teacher was instantly fired. They were apologetic and ashamed that this had happened at their daycare. This was a state-licensed facility and certified with the National Association for the Education of Young Children (NAEYC). We were understandably very upset over this and asked many questions and asked mainly if Isabella was OK. The school assured us she was and when we picked her up, she didn't mention it or even seem bothered by it. So our child was fine and while it was a bad situation, we didn't lose our heads over it. I told my mother, who works in child care, and she said it's terrible but the school handled it properly.

Now comes Act II. I told my wife not to tell her mother. She didn't listen. I may as well have said, "Don't go to Crystal Lake. There's a maniac with a hockey mask killing horny teenagers." She went to Crystal Lake. She told her mother. As I predicted, her mother freaked out and called my wife's entire family, and Audge was getting calls about how she should fight for her daughter and if it was *their* daughter they would march in there, yell, and cause a scene. This I found instantly both annoying and amusing. It obviously had no constructive purpose and in reality if someone is really upset, they cause a scene because they are upset and yelling. No one deliberately thinks, "I'm going to specifically cause some type of scene." You may as well be saying, "I'm going to deliberately show people I am out of my mind through a creative usage of yelling, threatening, and intricate arm movements."

This loud, verbal chastisement of my wife's sane and correct reaction to the incident of course made my wife feel even worse, and simply served no other purpose. Because something constructive always comes out of someone yelling like a lunatic and causing a scene, right? That doesn't even happen on a VH1 reality show. Eventually even Bret Michaels is going to throw you out of the house. But unfortunately, it got worse.

Audge's mother convinced her that she should "reenact" the incident with Isabella to get more information. I saw Audge do this and immediately put a stop to it. This got me very angry. First of all, in Isabella's head this was a minor incident and easily forgotten. She didn't even cry. When Audge re-enacted the slap on poor Isabella's hand like some History Channel show and asked if the teacher had done this to her, she got very quiet.

Now it was becoming a bigger, more memorable incident, because of my wife's actions. I could see it in Isabella's little eyes. She knew something was wrong, didn't really know what, but felt that *she* had done something wrong. Like somehow she had done something to feel ashamed of and was being bad.

Once I explained this to my wife, she immediately stopped. Then she felt bad. Then we both talked about how truly crazy her mother was. Or maybe I just did that in my head; I don't remember.

Every generation does things differently and however accepted at the time, in hindsight things are going to look pretty crazy. One of the interesting things about having family visit when you have a new baby is that they reminisce about when *you* were a child. My family would bring up things that I really didn't want to know about or had thankfully blocked out through a psychological defense mechanism.

For instance, we were talking about bassinets and my mom casually mentioned that when I was a child and they were downstairs, they just put me in a doll's crib. After confirming the authenticity of this statement, I was amazed at the casualness of this revelation. As ridiculous as this was to hear, I was struck more by the completely blasé way she said it, like putting a baby in a doll's crib was the most normal thing in the world, and that the people who put babies in people cribs were the crazy ones. I guess back then everything was made of wood and painted with lead paint, so what did it matter? Why not just put a baby in a cardboard box with the kittens?

Now I do want to give *you* some advice directly here, because I think it is very important. Sometimes life gets tough. Whether it's external or internal forces, we all go through shit sometimes. And a screaming child can be either the cause or the catalyst that can send you or your wife over the edge.

A friend of mine said she kind of lost it at one point when her daughter was driving her crazy with screaming, crying, and bad behavior. She put her daughter in the crib, ran out of the house with a little yelling of her own, and called her husband from the driveway. As crazy as this sounds, this is the *exact right thing to do*. If it ever gets too bad, *put the baby in a safe place, like his crib, and walk away*. Crying will not hurt your child. Call your spouse. Calm down. Push the reset button.

I read a news article that almost made me cry about babies who were shaken by frustrated parents and were now crippled, blind, or had died from their injuries. Never, ever, shake your baby. Please. *Never* go British Au Pair on your child.

OK, so that was some heavy shit, but I think it's something that every parent should understand. It's OK that you feel like you're overwhelmed and that it can be too much sometimes. We're all only human and we all have our breaking points. I'm sure one hot and humid day in Calcutta even Mother Teresa said to a kid, "For the love of God, just shut up and sit down!"

Keep in mind too that your infant won't be an infant forever. They will grow, become toddlers, and give you an all-new learning curve. But it will be different every time, from infancy to high school. There will be new joys and new challenges. It's still all about stages.

So who knows what is best for your child? The answer is obvious: *you* do. You're in tune with what his likes, dislikes, and even what his strengths and weaknesses are. Listen to your child. Take all the advice with a grain of salt and use what works and discard what doesn't. Remember, early on it's really only feed, change, play, sleep. That's it. It's like you're taking care of the Rolling Stones.

26

What's the Best and Worst Part About Having a Child?

So what makes them so great, anyway? Everyone says how magical having kids is. But what exactly is it that makes having a child so amazing? I think I know. And if you're reading this after your wife has given birth, you probably know now too.

Unlike us soiled, tarnished, and imperfect adults, children are innocent, pure, and full of light. Whatever you believe in, when you have a child, you feel like you're getting a glimpse of something divine. Whether you thank God, Nature, or a head of lettuce named Ralph, you know you should thank *someone*. This sounds incredibly contrived if you don't have children; I'm aware of that. It's like looking at a picture of the Sistine Chapel. Sure, it's beautiful. But once you actually travel to Rome and stand inside it, then you actually *understand*. Or if you saw the original *Star Wars* for the first time on a DVD at home or in a packed movie theater in 1977. You know what I'm talking about.

Children are a blank slate. They have what I call a *purity of expression*. They experience pure joy, and pure sadness. When they smile and laugh at you, it's like all the innocent joy in the world is looking straight at you. And when they cry, it's like it's the end of the world for them. And to them it is, because their world is so small.

When Isabella was happy and cooed, I felt happy. When Isabella was crying, I felt anxious and uneasy. Not just because it's loud and annoying. Because it was my child and she was experiencing discomfort. There was that bond, and when she felt bad, I felt bad. That bond will also get stronger and more complex with time.

A friend of mine once told me he couldn't have a kid because he thought having a kid would make him lose his childlike perspective and as a comedian he felt that's what made him a living. As crazy as that sounds, before I had a child, I thought there was some truth to that fear. Now, for all you childless comedians out there, you can relax. In reality, it's actually the opposite. Having a child *embraces* your inner child and you get to live your childhood all over again through their eyes. It's almost like taking a refresher course on childhood. You get to fill your house again with Dr. Seuss, army men, and animation DVDs. Actually, you never really got rid of that stuff, did you?

Although I have to say games like Cootie and Don't Break the Ice seemed a lot more fun when I was a kid. Now they're pretty boring. Of course, I didn't have a Play-Station back then either. Mouse Trap, however, is still pretty cool and Concentration seems *way* harder now.

So we don't lose our inner child. What we do lose is our "inner teenager" who is going out and getting drunk and trying to get laid at parties. That guy is being replaced by being in bed by 10:00 p.m., staying home on Saturday night, and trying to figure out how to get the DVR to re-cord *Dragon Tales*. But at this point, would you really miss him? Sure, he was fun to hang out with for a while but now he's just kind of pathetic. Let him go.

When I was anxious about having a child, I just kept thinking about what I was going to lose. Not what I was going to gain. I couldn't do *this* anymore. I couldn't do *that* anymore. No more going to the movies or out to din-ner. No more time alone. No more romantic getaways. No more skydiving lessons. No more turning my house into a brothel to get money for college when my parents went away. No wait, that was *Risky Business*.

A child doesn't destroy your life. He adds to it. The joy

of having a child makes up for anything you may lose. And with relatives and babysitters, you're still going to get to go out. You're not chained to the bed. Unless you want to be, and in that case you should probably do that in a hotel room away from your kids anyway. Let me put it another way: You don't *lose* things when you have a child. Having a child *adds* to your life; it does not take away. Sure, it adds all sorts of stuff. Mostly good and a few things bad, but the math still comes out as "greater than."

So we get to the ultimate question: *When you have a child, is your life over, or is it just beginning?* Well, neither, actually. You've already been here for a while, doing whatever it is that you do. And if what you do is telemarketing, then please stop ignoring the Do Not Call List and quit fucking calling me.

The thing is, when you have a child, your life *changes*. And it changes in almost every way. From your perspective on things to the way you spend your time. And this is a good thing. Having a child *should* change you. That's the whole point, isn't it?

A child gives you perspective. You forget about all the bullshit in your life when your child runs to you and gives you a big hug and the biggest smile you've ever seen in your life. Suddenly that jerk at work doesn't seem so important. In fact, he seems more pathetic than anything. OK, so slashing his tires is on hold. For now.

You also begin to realize the reason why some people are complete assholes. It really boils down to two things: fear and loneliness. People who are unafraid and have loved ones around them are generally pretty laid back. If you're in constant fear of losing your job, not paying a bill, and dying alone, of course you're going to be an asshole. Don't get me wrong, an asshole is still an asshole, but now it just doesn't matter anymore. No matter how much they try and make your life miserable, ultimately it's their problem and not yours.

All the bullshit in your life, what you've done and what's been done to you, it all melts away and you feel better about everything when you see the innocence, wonder, and love in your child's eyes. It's pure. It's genuine. It's the greatest thing in the world. Feel the love and the warmth of that child in your arms. A child has the ability to *heal* you. Let him.

Shortly after my daughter Isabella was born, I stopped taking Zoloft. I've never gone back. I haven't had to. I still take a sedative or two when the mother-in-law comes to visit, but no one can blame me for that. My wife has even dipped into that goody bag a few times herself.

So what's the worst part about having a child?

Sure, that's a heading you don't normally see in a child-care book. But it is a legitimate question. And for me and

I think most men, since we are so freaked out about having the child in the first place, it's not something we think about right away. We think about not going out anymore, changing diapers, never sleeping again, having throw up on everything, not being able to get drunk on Friday nights, blacking out and waking up in an alley Saturday morning with a suitcase full of rough-cut diamonds handcuffed to our wrist. As it turns out, those things never rise higher than annoyances. They really don't. The scary stuff about having children really wasn't so scary.

But there is one thing that is scary, and here it is: *The worst part about having a child is the constant worry that something bad is going to happen to him.* There it is; that's it. You can relax now. Simple enough, right? It only intrudes into every waking and sleeping thought you have, but other than that no big deal.

I remember waking up in the middle of the night playing the unwinnable "what if?" game. What if Isabella falls off the swing? What if she pokes her eye out with a pool cue? What if she falls off the roof? (How she got there is irrelevant.) What if in the middle of the night, during the winter solstice, she's carried off by a pack of werewolves who are afraid she's the Chosen One who will one day grow up and destroy them? The last thing you want to deal with as a parent is a pack of angry, vengeful werewolves. Try going to Babies "R" Us and asking for pacifiers and silver bullets because of a prophecy. OK, maybe I got a little carried away. I doubt she's going to fall off the swing. Those things have straps.

But it never ends. I was worried about her falling out of the crib. Then falling off the bed, then hurting herself with a pitchfork, bee stings, car accidents, daycare accidents, unsafe jungle gyms, the germ-filled mall, toys with small parts that look tasty, pricking her finger on a spinning needle, lead paint from China, babysitters with secret heroin addictions, etc. I started thinking it was a wonder any kid survived.

When you think about it, it's a wonder *we* survived. Every once in a while my mother or father will say something or do something that makes me think I could not have possibly just heard or seen that. For instance, one time my family was visiting from back east and we decided to take a few days and drive up to San Luis Obispo. I said we would need two cars. My father suggested we all pile in his rental car since it was bigger. I said there's no car seat for Isabella. He replied, "We'll just take turns holding her." Pause. No response came to mind, even for me. Some things you just need to block out, and it immediately made me wonder what else I had blocked out over the years when I was growing up. I have a few scars on my body that no one seems to want to talk about.

So the best and worst parts of having a child will continue to evolve and become quite personal for you. Soon you and your wife will amass a library of memories to share and reminisce about. Then when your child gets older, you can reminisce with him about the ups and downs and the mistakes you've made. You can relive all of the nostalgic moments of urgent care visits and unexpected allergies as your now older child's face grows more and more ashen. See? You're paying it forward.

27

Other than the Robots Taking Over, What Does the Future Hold?

I couldn't think about having a child without thinking about the future. Now every time I look at my daughter, I feel like I can actually see the future. There it is, right in front of me, the future, staring at me and wishing I would give it some chocolate. What's in store? School, middle school, dance classes, dating, college, paying for college—you know what, I need to calm down. So what *does* the future hold? All I can say is, I have absolutely no idea. And unless you're that guy from *The Dead Zone*, then neither will you.

But I do know that everything starts with you. Yes, I'm going to get all philosophical here. It's the last chapter, so bear with me. Your child will initially learn everything from you. So let me drop a little Zen on you: Now that it's not all about you, it's all about you. Ooooh, deep.

Your adventures in child raising start with the type of person *you* are. Are you happy? Miserable? Nervous? Anxious? You are the first lens through how your child will view the world. Show by example. (Again, that same advice.) Be happy. Don't scream at your wife or child. Even when they get mouthy. Be responsive to your child's needs. But don't spoil her. You do your child no favors if you let her do whatever she wants without consequence. Do you really want to be like that mother whose teenage daughter is screaming at her in the mall? Even that mother doesn't want to be that mother.

Keep in mind your child will observe not only how you treat him or her, but how he sees you treat *other people* as well. Kids observe and see. How are you treating her mother? Happy children come from happy homes. Not always, but why not put everything in their favor?

Children *feel* anger and tension when it's in the house, even when it's not directed at them. I remember once my brother and father were visiting. They had left and a few minutes later my wife said, "Do you know the door to our house is wide open?" When my brother and father left, they had *forgotten* to close the front door to our house. What was worse is we have an indoor cat and she got out. Luckily I found her under our car and brought her back in the house. I was furious, and rightfully so, yelling and saying all sorts of unprintable things. But then in the middle of my . . . tantrum . . . my wife looked at me and was holding our daughter. Isabella was crying. She was crying because I was yelling and I don't normally yell. And I certainly wasn't yelling at her. But it didn't matter. She was crying and upset, only because she saw that I was being loud and angry. I calmed down and held her, and the next day my father and brother apologized. But we have a rule now that they have to be walked to the door anytime they leave our house. Like children.

As your children get older, treat them like people. After all, that's all they are, just little people without knowledge or experience. Don't treat them like property or pets and don't expect them to act like it. As they get older, they will not necessarily fit into your vision of them. That's fine. You want your child to have his own vision, and it may not always involve you.

The best quote I ever read about parenting was this famous quote by author Hodding Carter:

> *"There are two lasting bequests we can give our children: One is roots, the other is wings."*

Now, what the hell does this mean? You've heard this quote, but no one ever quotes the explanation:

"A child who knows he's loved unconditionally is a child with roots, he'll stand in the storms of life. On the other hand, give him self-worth and teach him to dream, and you'll give him wings."

I interpreted it in an even broader sense. Roots not only help your child stand strong, but strong family roots mean he'll never forget where he comes from, and it will be important to him, as it should be. Then when the roots are strong, so is the child and he will be ready to leave the nest and fly on his own. And he should be encouraged to do so. Of course, I wonder if Hodding Carter's parents may have made some mistakes along the way. After all, they did name him "Hodding."

You're going to make mistakes too. There's no getting around it. Until Skynet takes over or we're all replaced by body-snatching pods, human beings are going to make mistakes. I remember going crazy over little things, even worse than my wife. We all got caught out in the rain one day and that night Isabella woke up with croup. I blamed myself and was so angry about it, it actually slowed me down from calling the doctor in the middle of the night and getting a prescription. The important thing is that you learn from your mistakes and every once in a while, give yourself a break. Having a child is difficult, and there is no such thing as a perfect parent. Only a good, loving one. So be a good, loving parent and leave the perfection and inevitable human subjugation to the robots.

So while you're learning from your own mistakes, help your children learn from theirs. Teach your children. Talk to them, but listen too. Give them values. Nurture them but give them boundaries. When you've done all you can, let them fly. Oftentimes you'll find that they will not only fly, but soar.

Look forward to the whole process. I am. It's a constantly changing affair. Rolling over, crawling, walking, talking, etc. It happens quickly, but not *that* quickly. I am looking forward to Isabella going to school and eventually making her own way in life. Am I looking forward to every little thing? Of course not. Only a crazy person would. I'm not looking forward to the teenage years and the speeches of "I hate you, you never let me do anything," etc. It's probably not going to be like *Sixteen Candles*, but hope and delusion spring eternal. But these stages are necessary, and while you are not looking forward to them, you'll want them to occur. Your child needs to test the boundaries or she'll never grow. You'll be a punching bag and a safety net. Sometimes in the same day. So wear something comfortable.

There's nothing like having a child. Nothing at all in your life will ever compare to it. So enjoy these very special moments. When you boil it down, our whole lives are really just made up of a series of defining moments. A lot of them involve our children. Although some of them do not, and some of them you keep to yourself. But when you look back on your life, it will be like a highlight reel and your most defining moments will play out over and over. The moments with your children will be first and at the top of your list. The highlights of the highlight reel.

I remember my daughter was less than a year old and was just learning to sit up on her own. She was sitting on my lap and unexpectedly looked at me and smiled. It was one of those moments. She seemed to be saying, "I'm glad you're my daddy." I hope she never loses that look in her eyes.

ACKNOWLEDGMENTS

The most obvious thank you goes to my wife of infinite patience, Audrey, and my precious and precocious daughter, Isabella, without whom this book would not have been possible. Literally. Audrey is the bestest wife ever, and also a great (and brutally honest) reader.

I would also like to thank my agents, Michael Ebeling and Kristina Holmes, who took a real interest in me and my work. An extra special shout out to my most awesome editor Patrick Price and the team at Simon Spotlight Entertainment. In addition to paying me, Patrick is a real joy to work with. Not only did he take a chance on a first-time author, he is the type of development person that writers hope for. One that helps the artist find his voice, and then makes it louder. And Patrick, I apologize in advance if after this acknowledgment you get flooded with new submissions.

I want to acknowledge author, comedienne, and friend Stefanie Wilder-Taylor for giving me inspiration and invaluable help and feedback. Not to mention the cool foreword.

I also wish to thank my family and my wife's family for the extra material. Seriously, your support has always been appreciated as well.

Thanks also to my various sounding boards, including Neil T. Weakley, Derek Guiley, and Chris and Ally Loprete over at ourmilkmoney.com for feedback and letting me try out this whole blogging thing.

Last but not least, I'd like to thank you, the discerning consumer, for purchasing this book or at least receiving it as a gift or stealing it from someone who purchased it. Cool.

ABOUT THE AUTHOR

A comic and a filmmaker, Chris Mancini has screened and spoken at various prestigious festivals including Slamdance, HBO's U.S. Comedy Arts Festival and at Comic-Con in San Diego. His short film compilation DVD *Myopic Visions* is out now. Chris is also a regular on Budd Friedman's world-famous Improv Comedy Club circuit. You can often find him trolling around the Internet at his blog *Daddy Needs Some Alone Time* or at comedyfilmnerdsdotcom.com. Chris lives in a hovering heli-carrier somewhere over Los Angeles with his wife, Audrey, his daughter, Isabella, his new son, Griffin, and their unusually white cat, Avatar.